PTSD and ME

By

Richard M. Czop, MD

Chapbook Press

Schuler Books
2660 28th Street SE
Grand Rapids, MI 49512
(616) 942-7330
www.schulerbooks.com

ISBN 13: 9781943359080

Library of Congress Control Number: 2015948698

Copyright © 2015 Richard Czop
All rights reserved.

No part of this book may be reproduced in any form without express permission of the copyright holder.

Printed in the United States by Chapbook Press.

DEDICATION

This book is dedicated to my wife Cathie; Thomas C. McGillen, the strongest man I have ever known; to all other combat veterans and their families.

INTRODUCTION

All people find themselves in danger or feel threatened at some time in their lives, and they function to the best of their ability in those circumstances. For combat soldiers, threat is continuous and ultimate, i.e. their own and their buddies' lives are on the line. Their training is rigorous, thorough, and ongoing; the goal of it is to maximize the ability to recognize and respond to threat. Implicit in the process is the willingness to temporarily suspend every law and religious teaching relating to the taking of a human life which applied to them as civilians. The end result is a change in the set points for what is perceived as threatening and what will be done to control or eliminate it.

War experiences become a permanent part of a person and can have cognitive and behavioral consequences, some obvious and predictable, others more subtle and unexpected. I either did not know those facts, or I drastically underestimated how they might impact my life subsequent to serving as a medic with the 9th Infantry Division in Vietnam in 1969. My personality makeup had a lot to do with it, but the nature of the combat seen in Vietnam, and in most military engagements since, made a significant contribution. Desert Storm was somewhat of an exception. The buildup to the actual battle resembled the World Wars: the mission was clearly defined, supported by a large number of nations, and the enemy forces were readily identifiable. It differed in that the application of modern weapons technology facilitated the conclusion of it in weeks rather than years. Targets ranging from individual enemy soldiers to massive installations could be identified using space-based satellites. Incredibly lethal types and amounts of ordinance could be launched from ships, submarines, aircraft (some unmanned), and vehicles on the ground, and guided on computer screens to remote targets with laser precision. The war was concluded with astonishingly few casualties on the winning side, and the major face-to-face interactions between opposing forces occurred when thousands of enemy troops surrendered.

In the process, George H. W. Bush restored America's confidence in our government and its ability to conduct an effective, large scale military intervention and "win." As a Vietnam veteran, I was relieved, grateful, and reassured: America had learned from its mistakes and would not repeat them.

Sadly, subsequent military interventions have looked more like Vietnam, the dirty war, than Desert Storm. Dirty wars often evolve from the fundamentally flawed premise that beliefs can be killed by bullets and bombs. They are intensely personal, usually prolonged, and produce no significant alteration in civilian life neither while they are being fought nor after they are over. They are not formally "declared," and they never really end; they just go on for a while and then they aren't there anymore. Their duration is determined by periods of time – tours, activations, deployments - not by the actual achievement of some honorable, well-defined military objective. An attempt is made to blunt their impact on the psyche by using less harsh terminology to describe them. We don't send soldiers into kill-or-be-killed situations; we put them in "harm's way." The inevitable killing of innocent civilians – men, women, and children – is referred to as "collateral damage." The most significant changes brought about by dirty wars occur in the hearts and minds of the people called upon to fight them.

I used to believe that combat-related psychological problems were confined to those soldiers who had served the longest, participated in, or witnessed, the most killing and mutilation, or who had sustained the worst permanent physical damage. They were the expressionless bearded men with major depression and superimposed drug and/or alcohol issues sitting around in VA facilities, local shelters, or in the streets of major cities.

I couldn't have problems: my tour was cut short, I never faced an enemy force of any size, and my physical wounds healed without being obvious to others. I came home, became a medical doctor, built a family, and had a good career. All the while I dealt with psychological and emotional consequences of my participation in war that I denied existed and for which I refused to get help. In the process, my family suffered in silence.

I could be wrong, but I don't think I'm unique. I believe there are other veterans like me: permanently changed and in need of help at times, but embarrassed or afraid to speak up because they are not amputees participating in triathlons, were not highly decorated soldiers, or because they have nice homes, good jobs, and look okay to everybody else. It has been difficult and taken a long time, but I have come to understand that "moving on" is not about doing your best to forget what happened. That will never occur. The key is forgiving yourself for what you had to do, what you should have done, and above all for surviving.

Is it easier for today's volunteer armed forces veterans? I think it's harder. People don't like to admit it, but deep inside they take some solace in thinking today's soldier "asks for" whatever happens. Chances are good that the average person does not have a close relative or friend on active duty in a combat zone. They are saddened to some degree by reports of American soldiers wounded or killed in action, but they do not feel the deep and intense pain of the victims' next of kin and a relatively small circle of their friends. The average person's life is not changed. They do not have to attend a funeral or memorial service, or restructure *their* life to care for a seriously disabled veteran for the rest of *his or her* life. They feel no compulsion to actively protest or even seriously question the decisions that commit American soldiers to combat.

I struggled with writing this story for many years. Pen and paper were the safest tools to use in dealing with the wide range of emotions I experienced at certain times. When I decided what I had to say might be beneficial to others, there were risks that needed to be weighed. Were the problems just mine? Would I embarrass myself or my family? In addition, I believed I had reason to fear retaliation by the United States Department of Justice.

When the 4000th combat death in Iraq wasn't enough of a stimulus to make me overcome my fear of negative personal consequences and act, I began to feel weak, ashamed, and depressed – a recurrent problem through the years. It took being diagnosed with prostate cancer, an Agent Orange-related condition, to reset my priorities. I hope what I share will help other veterans. We owe it to ourselves, our families, and others around us to understand and accept that there may be times when we have problems dealing with past combat experiences.

Finally, I want to say to all Veterans, "Welcome home, and thank you for your service."

PART ONE

CHAPTER 1

July, 1968

I was determined to be a good soldier. After Basic Training at Fort Knox, Kentucky, I was sent to Fort Sam Houston, the Army Medical Training Center in San Antonio, Texas, for AIT (Advanced Individual Training). On a Sunday afternoon just past the halfway point in the program, I made my weekly call home. My mom said my father and brother were fine, but she sounded a little strange, so after a few minutes of basic conversation, I asked her what was wrong.

"Richard, I have bad news."

With my family being okay, how bad could it be?

"Tommy's been wounded again."

"I wasn't ready to hear that; he was my best friend. This was the third time. After the second, I quit school and volunteered for the draft.

"Is he dead?" I finally got out.

"No."

I let go a sigh of relief. When you're not dead, you're fixable. I was ready for the details.

"How bad, Ma?"

"He's paralyzed from the neck down."

I could not speak. She proceeded to give me the few details anyone had. The Army or the Red Cross had sent a telegram to his folks informing them he was somewhere between Vietnam and Walter Reed Army Hospital in Washington, DC. His neck was broken, and he was paralyzed.

"Don't you go volunteering to go over there. You can't do anything to change what's happened. You'll only get yourself hurt."

She was right, but I had to do something.

"I don't think orders for my next assignment have been cut yet. I'm going to see if maybe I can get stationed at Walter Reed or nearby so I can help take care of him."

I knew I was in the Army. It was a longshot, but it couldn't hurt to ask, and it gave us something positive and hopeful to think about, but I still cried on the bus all the way back to Fort Sam.

I went to the orderly room on Monday morning and told the company commander what happened and why I was there. Captain Howard shuffled paper on his desk without making eye contact then informed me that orders for our next assignments were already cut and could not be changed. I said I understood and thanked him for his time.

After we were dismissed for the weekend that Saturday, I called Tom, who had undergone surgery to stabilize his neck fractures earlier that morning. I hadn't talked to him in ten months; I needed to hear his voice. He said he was in pain, paralyzed, but okay because he was still alive. I just told him I was praying for him, and I would come see him as soon as AIT was over.

I was overwhelmed with grief and helplessness; I went from the phone booth directly to the Training Center Administrative Office across the street. I was greeted at the reception desk by the Officer of the Day, and I told him about Tom and that I just wanted to make sure there was no way I could get stationed near him. He was compassionate and understanding, and he confirmed the orders were cut and beyond being changed. He said he was sorry about that and about Tom's wounds and said Tom was a hero. His kindness helped me get through the weekend.

Monday morning, I was called out of formation and sent to the company orderly room. I felt a surge of hope as I was ushered in to see the executive officer, Lt. Pembrook.

"What do you mean barging in on the center's Officer-of-the-Day and demanding to have your orders changed?" he said to me.

I told him what actually had taken place. I don't know if he heard me or not.

"You are being subjected to disciplinary action for going out of the chain of command. You are restricted to the company area, you will sign in hourly in this orderly room every day after training until lights out, and if you continue to disregard regulations, further disciplinary action will follow. That's all."

I stood there dumbfounded.

"You are dismissed. Join your company."

Over the next couple of weeks, I stopped talking, lost weight, and started getting into fights. Several friends who had been in basic with me were concerned and talked to a guy who lived in our barracks and worked as a clerk in the orderly room.

On a Monday morning, I was again called out of formation, only this time I was to go to the battalion orderly room. I figured there'd be a firing squad there, but when I arrived, the first sergeant was pleasant and ushered me in to the battalion commander, Major Wood. I stood at attention and saluted.

"At ease, son. Have a seat. I understand you're having a problem in your company. Can you tell me about it?"

I was relieved but still leery as I told him what had taken place.

"Do you mean to tell me that they put you on restriction for this?" he asked.

"Yes, Sir," I answered.

He pressed a button on his intercom.

"First Sergeant, get this man's company on the phone and have him removed from restriction immediately, and explain to them that there is an open-door policy on this base so anyone with a problem like this can see anyone they feel they need to see. Am I clear?"

"Yes, Sir," the voice on the intercom responded.

My jaw dropped open. He turned back to me.

"Now where did you say your friend was?"

"He's at Walter Reed Army Hospital Neurosurgical unit, Sir."

"Let's see how he is doing."

He picked up the phone, and within minutes, he was talking to

Tom.

"Your friend here at Fort Sam has told me about you, and I just want you to know it is an honor for me to talk to you. Rich is very concerned about you, and so am I. How are you coming along?"

Major Wood listened and said "good" a couple of times after pauses.

"Well, I'm glad you're feeling better. Why don't you talk to your friend and tell him, too."

When he handed me the phone, I nearly dropped it. I thought I must be dreaming. Tom sounded better. He even got a laugh out of my being in a major's office.

"Knowing you, I'm not surprised," he said.

Then we wrapped it up, and I gave back the phone.

"Come back Wednesday, and we'll give him another call."

After AIT, about half the company was going right over to Vietnam; I was going back to Fort Knox to work at Ireland Army Hospital. As I was about to leave the barracks, I saw Gary Jones, one of my favorite people in AIT, sitting on his bunk with he hands on his face looking down at the floor. He was married and had a kid and he was going to Vietnam. I went over to him.

"Gary, I'm sorry."

"Me, too, but thanks," he answered.

"I'd go in your place if they'd let me," I told him.

He looked up at me for a second.

"I know you would, Rich. I can see it all now, you walking into headquarters and saying you want different orders again."

We laughed; it took away some of the hurt.

"I hope we run into each other when this is all over," I said.

"I'd like that a lot," he answered.

We shook hands for a long time and then said goodbye.

I left AIT as an honor graduate, fourth in my class of five-hundred forty. The most important lesson I learned was not part of the curriculum: I saw the kind of leader a soldier would walk into hell with gasoline drawers on to serve, and I came to understand why in combat, "fragging" an officer perceived by his men as a threat to their survival could occur.

　　It was good to be home with my family again. I stayed around long enough to book a flight to DC.　I stood inside the door of the Neurosurgical Unit. On each side of the wide center aisle was a row of beds of different kinds, ranging from standard hospital beds, to circular extravaganzas that could rotate full circle head to foot, and others that could be flipped over side to side after a top piece was securely bolted on. A few of the patients could sit up in bed or in a wheelchair next to it.

　　I started down the aisle looking at faces, some of which were looking back, some of which could only look straight up at the ceiling or straight down at the floor because they were in frames or traction. One man had a deformity in his forehead not unlike a dent in a Ping-Pong ball. He sat there okay, but his expression was blank, and his gaze did not follow me as I walked across his field of vision. He made no sound. Another was sitting in a wheelchair with his head between four posts of a brace. There was a lit cigarette in the ashtray on his tray table, and as I went by, he asked me to please help him take a drag. I picked it up and held it out for him to take, but his arms and legs didn't work anymore. I had to hold it to his lips so he could take deep enough puff to last him until someone else passed by.

　　Before long I had reached the far end of the ward and had not seen him. I started walking back to the desk at the entrance when I recognized a pair of feet with oversized first toes. My eyes moved up the body to the head, which had tongs stuck in just behind the temples. A rope attached the tongs to some weights that kept a gentle, steady pull on the neck of my best friend.

　　"Hi, Tom," I forced out.

　　"Hey, how're ya doin'?" he answered.

　　"Just a minute," I said. "It's a little warm in here for me. I'll be right back."

"Okay, I ain't goin' anywhere."

I made it out to the hall, took some deep breaths, and leaned against the wall. I thought I was about to pass out, and I looked for a good place to land. After a minute or two, I got a drink from a fountain and started to feel better. I didn't want him to think that I had gotten sick because of how he looked, so I took a deep breath, walked briskly back through the doors, and we got right into it.

"Why in the hell did you quit school and go into the service, asshole? Do you want to wind up like this?" he asked.

"You were ugly before you went over there," I answered, "and once you heal up, you'll be all right and I'll beat your ass as usual."

That broke the ice and we batted it back and forth for about an hour. When they brought his food, I said I was starved, too, and had to take off and find a side of beef or something and I'd be back later.

"Bring me a malt will ya," he called after me?

"Sure," I shouted back over my shoulder.

Back in my room, I collapsed on the bed. I could no more eat than I could stop crying; I left because I couldn't stand to watch him being fed his lunch. It would have been easier to accept that he had been killed, rather than to have him so drastically changed. Images flooded my brain. The longest time I had ever seen him perfectly still was waiting for the puck to drop for a faceoff, the next snap of the football, the release of a free throw, or the swing of a golf club.

I remembered the last time I had seen him. He was leaving for Vietnam the next morning. I took my gold Saint Christopher Medal off my neck and put it on his, and he gave me a hand-written copy of a prayer from a holy card.

In Vietnam, he commanded an armored personnel carrier and had been all over the Central Highlands with the 4th Infantry Division. He was there for the worst of the war (including the 1968 Tet Offensive), fought against the toughest of enemy units (NVA regulars, not just the Viet Cong), and in the closest of combat situations, including hand-to-hand. He got malaria and had been wounded two other times. What he saw and did would give him nightmares for the rest of his life.

A soldier from Tom's unit sent his family a letter about what happened; otherwise, we would have never known. His track drove over a land mine made from a five-hundred pound American bomb that failed to detonate. The enemy had recovered it, rigged it with a detonator, and buried it in a dirt road. Someone hidden nearby triggered the blast that sent Tom fifty feet in the air, and he landed on the back of his neck. One member of his crew lost his legs in the explosion, and another went bonkers because of what he witnessed. Tom has no recollection of the event.

"I'm going to come back from this," he said between sips of the malt as I held the straw.

"I don't care what they say. I'll do whatever it takes to walk again, no matter how long or how hard I have to work."

If anyone could, it would be him. His spirit and attitude would optimize whatever outcome was ahead.

When it came time for me go home, Tom broke the silence.

"Rich, what's done is done." He paused. "This isn't anybody's fault, and you can't fix it."

I couldn't have answered even if I could think of something to say. I looked at his face; his eyes were wet.

"I know what you're thinking; don't do it. Don't go over there. It really is hell, and it's not worth it."

"Okay," I mumbled.

"I mean it. Your mom will kill me if you get hurt."

"Okay. Don't sweat it," I said.

Finally, I got up.

"I got to catch a plane. I'll be back when I get a few day's leave. You take it easy, huh?"

"I mean it," he said again.

I reached for his hand and gave it a reassuring squeeze. I forgot that he couldn't feel it.

As I drove back across town to the airport, I wanted to get out of the car and scream, "Hey, you bastards. You made a war, took my buddy, used him, and you fucked him up. He was your basic American kid, but you made him a soldier, and now he's something called a quad in a room with a bunch of other quads, and all for what?"

They were sons, husbands, and fathers. To the U.S. Army, they were "personnel wounded in action." I had always thought of WIA's as people who got hurt and then got better, not the guys on that ward. There they were, a few of the 500,000 policy implementers, and nearby were the people who made the laws and justified the war. Somewhere half-a-world away was a place where it all played out.

The scenes flashing by outside intensified the pain and anger I was feeling. The gutted, charred, and crumbling remains of some of the buildings torched in the aftermath of the death of Martin Luther King Jr. still stood in stark contrast to nearby white marble memorials of bygone eras. After King, Robert Kennedy was shot dead moments after he acknowledge his victory in the crucial California Presidential Primary. Any hope I had that America could find its way forward again would shortly be erased.

The last week of my leave, my parents and I watched the Democratic National Convention on television. The Peace and Freedom Party's Eldridge Cleaver fortunately drew limited support for his "kill whites" platform. The Yippies wanted to nominate a live pig, but it got itself arrested. One-hundred anti-war groups came to Chicago under the coordination of the National Mobilization Committee to End the War in Vietnam. The confrontation that occurred outside the convention was unforgettably ugly. Riot police flailed away, with equal justice for bystander and activist alike, bashing heads in the streets to protect the rights of those inside to assemble, release balloons, and sing "Happy Days Are Here

Again."

Ireland Army Hospital at Fort Knox was a four-hundred bed facility where soldiers whose home towns were within a couple-hundred-mile radius were sent after being wounded in Vietnam. I was assigned to the orthopedic ward. Orthopedic cases in the Army tended to spend a fair amount of time in the hospital before they were ready to return to some semblance of duty or be discharged from the service. They talked with each other and with the staff about their war experiences, glibly and with bravado at first, but as they hung around, the full emotional toll of combat became more apparent. Their time here helped them transition from the war to being home. They came and went; I stayed. On my arrival at Fort Knox, I began submitting the paperwork volunteering to go to Vietnam. Every month a list came out with the names of who was being transferred there. After seven months of waiting, my name finally appeared. I had a leave before I would be departing.

"I've been waiting for you to show up so I could beat your ass."

With that, Tom lifted the armrest off his wheelchair and waved it like a club.

"If you couldn't do it before, you damn sure ain't going to now," I teased.

He was in the latter stages of his nine-month rehabilitation program at Cleveland Veteran's Hospital. When he first got there, they told him that he could either quit or work to improve whatever function he had left to become as independent as he could. He was down for a while, but then he became an inspiration to everyone around him. He would be going home soon, and he told me about his plans to finish college.

"Of course, I can revise those if Michael Anthony shows up with the check," he wrapped the conversation up with. We both laughed. We hadn't thought about late 1950's TV series, The Millionaire, for a long time. We used to tell people we were going wait for Michael Anthony to bring the check instead of working for a living. It was good to laugh again, and we did a lot of that during the visit. I was there two days, and just as I was about to leave, he asked me to do something.

"Can you get me that brown bag in the drawer over there?" he asked.

I found it and gave it to him. He worked his hand inside and was trying to get something out.

"Need a hand?" I offered.

"Got two of my own," he came back.

Tough bastard, I thought to myself. He started withdrawing his hand from the bag.

"Here," he said reaching out toward me. "You're gonna need this. You'll have to put it on."

Into my hand he dropped my gold St. Christopher medal. I looked at it for a few seconds.

"I guess it didn't work very well."

"Bullshit!" he answered. "I came back and I'm not done. Put it on."

The living wake was over. I had said goodbye to my relatives at a reunion in Garfield, New Jersey. Now it was just my mother and father and I. We had kept it light during most of the ride to Fort Dix. My father had left for World War II from here. We talked about some of the things he recognized, and that made it easier. Then the moment we tried not to think about for the past month arrived: time to say goodbye for what could be the last time. We hugged, kissed, and there were some tears. I don't remember exactly what we said, but I will never forget their faces as they mirrored the pain they were feeling. They had said goodbye to each other on this spot twenty-seven years earlier. Dad was one of the lucky ones. I hoped for their sake I would follow in his footsteps, but deep inside I had a sickening feeling that I would never see them again. I watched the car until it was out of sight then stood there, more alone than I had ever felt in my life.

CHAPTER 2

We got off the plane and onto a bus that took us to the Replacement Center at Long Binh, Republic of South Vietnam. A staff sergeant was organizing us into a formation when he was interrupted by a guy who rode up in a pickup truck and handed him a note. He read it and looked up.

"I need six B-positive blood donors right now. We got anybody with B-positive who could give a unit of blood?"

Six of us got into the back of the truck and were driven about a quarter mile to a small, fortified, windowless building. As we drove up, a helicopter was gently easing itself down onto a red "H" on the ground. People came running out of the building and began offloading stretchers bearing dirty, skinny GI's with most of their clothing gone and blood-soaked field dressings tied over multiple wounds on their bodies. One with his head wrapped in bloody bandages stumbled forward between two guys who could barely walk themselves. When people tried to help, they waved them away and refused to give up their buddy until they got him inside.

I stood there staring, feeling the wind from the spinning rotors and hearing that whomp-whomp sound that used to just mean helicopter but from that moment on would mean Vietnam, wherever and whenever I heard it. I was just twenty-four hours removed from the comfort and security of the "block" - a family reunion no less. I could still taste stuffed cabbage when I burped. Nothing in my training prepared me for what I felt at that moment. I squinted in the bright sun and wiped sweat from my forehead. Some of the guys being carried off that chopper were about to pay the ultimate price; some of those back in the formation I just left would replace them. When the chopper lifted off, we were led into the building. It was well-lit and air conditioned. Medical personnel surrounded the wounded who were still on their original stretchers which now rested on metal saw horses. I was impressed with how little sound there was. Everybody knew what to do; words were not necessary. I was witnessing the essence of war: young soldiers dying.

After a couple days each at progressively smaller bases processing in, I found myself being driven down a dirt road with nothing but rice paddies, an occasional vehicle which had been blown up by a mine, and patches of defoliated jungle. I thought with seven months experience as a corpsman on an orthopedic ward at Fort Knox, I would be assigned to a large or maybe medium-sized hospital facility. The driver sped from one side of the road to the other hoping to miss mines or minimize the impact if we hit one. After about twenty minutes, I yelled over the engine noise.

"How much farther is it to Bien Phouc?"

"There it is," he nodded into the distance.

I didn't see anything but a big fence, a couple of one-story buildings and a tower.

"You mean—"

"Yep, that's it. We call it 'Been Fucked.'"

On the outskirts of a tiny village was the base camp of the 2nd Battalion, 47th Infantry, 9th Infantry Division, also known as the Panthers - the only mechanized infantry unit operating in the Mekong Delta. Well, at least we would be on armored personnel carriers instead of walking, I thought to myself.

In the headquarters conference room, an officer gave me my orientation.

"Welcome. Do your job, and nobody will fuck with you. Don't be an asshole or a hero. Lastly, develop a great respect for the enemy. Questions?"

"No, Sir."

When I walked into the glorified bunker that served as the battalion aid station, I was stunned. The place had about eight to ten guys in it, most shirtless, and all clean and happy looking. Some were on a couch in front of a TV, some were at a table playing poker, and one was mixing drinks at a small bar. It was well lit, there were a couple of fans, it was clean, and it was dry. It may have been remote, but it was the warmest, friendliest, safest place I had seen in the country up to now.

I told the nearest guy who I was.

"Nice to meet you, toss your shit over there, hey, Top, your FNG (fucking new guy) is here," he shouted into the poker game.

After the hand in the poker game was over, a Japanese guy with no shirt came over, introduced himself, and shook my hand. He looked like he could kick Bruce Lee's ass.

"I'm First Sergeant Tara. Welcome to Bien Phouc."

He took me around and introduced me to everybody, then we sat down and he oriented me to the unit as a whole and my job in particular.

"Each of the infantry companies in the Battalion has three to four platoons and each has a medic. You'll be with B company third platoon. They're operating with another unit outside of Rach Kien about ten klicks from here. You'll hook up with them tomorrow. Till then, just hang out here and see what goes on."

"Okay, thanks."

Scattered around the facility were metal cages of various sizes and configurations with numbers on them.

"Somebody got hamsters?" I asked one of the guys.

"Those are rat traps. We build them and keep score on whose trap works best. That number on them is how many have been caught in that trap so far this rainy season."

The highest was seventy-four.

When it came time to sack out, I had no idea where I'd be sleeping until one of the guys opened up a stretcher and put it on the floor where the folding table for the poker game had been. He threw me a blanket and a pillow.

"You can sleep right there."

"Thanks."

"If we get mortared, stay here. This is the safest structure in the camp."

As I lay there, I tried to sort out how I had gone from being a junior in pre-med at Michigan State, a corpsman on an orthopedic ward in an Army hospital, to now being a medic in an infantry unit, a grunt. How and why did not matter anymore. One thing was clear: I had hit rock bottom. After I fell asleep, I was awakened by a cold, wet, sniff against my cheek. I smacked at it, and it galloped away. Could a rat be that big? I pulled my blanket over my head despite the heat. When morning came, everybody started moving about getting ready for sick call.

"Anybody seen Band-Aid?" one guy asked.

"Band-Aid!" somebody yelled.

Out from a corner crept this big, yellow hound with his head down and his tail between his legs. He had part of an army belt and buckle for a collar and a Combat Medic Badge pinned on it. The giant rat I slugged last night was the medical platoon's dog. I called him over and apologized and played with him a little bit. He started to wag his tail, and I swear he smiled. We became friends.

I hooked up with Bravo Company in Rach Kien the next day.

I immediately spotted a guy I recognized from home. We had played Little League baseball together and hadn't seen each other in years.

"Hey, Ron," I called to him.

"I don't believe this!" he said to me. "What are the chances? Wow! How are ya? What outfit are you in?"

"B company third platoon; I'm their new medic."

"I'm in the fourth platoon. Hey, do you know Eddie Kapp from the neighborhood? He's in the 4th, too"

He and his brother worked with my brother. I'd seen Eddie around but never met him. We had to come to Vietnam to do that.

"Are you shittin' me?" he said when Ron brought us together. We shook hands.

I answered with my new favorite word, "Unbelievable."

We talked for a few minutes, and then I told them I had to hook up with Doc Johnson, the senior medic. They took me to him and introduced me as a visiting friend from home.

"Small fucked up world, huh," Johnson laughed. "Let me get you ready for tomorrow. We're part of a search-and-clear mission in the morning."

He went through my aid bags and told me what I wouldn't need and what I needed more of. He also showed me how to carry them so they wouldn't look so much like aid bags.

"The VC like to shoot medics and officers because it fucks up everybody," he explained.

As I was thanking him, another guy walked up, and Johnson introduced us.

"Bill, this is Rich. He's your new medic. Rich, meet Bill Word, your platoon leader's radiotelephone operator, or RTO."

We exchanged greetings and shook hands.

"Word, can you take him around and introduce him to your guys? I got some stuff I have to do."

"Be glad to," he answered. "C'mon, Rich."

I didn't realize it then, but I had just basically been simultaneously adopted and given a second guardian angel.

"Mount up," somebody yelled from somewhere at the head of a line of nine idling tracks.

"Move out!"

Everyone's rifle clicked as we cleared the gate.

"Lock and load, Doc," the guy sitting next to me on top of the track said.

I chambered a round.

"Leave the safety on till you got something to shoot at," he cautioned.

"Okay thanks."

For what seemed like an hour, we drove through the paddies, slowed to a near stop to climb up and over the dikes, then repeated the drill over and over. Finally, we stopped and were looking at dense vegetation a few hundred yards away. Two F-4 Phantom jets appeared silently out of nowhere and started dropping bombs and napalm between two white smoke markers a piper cub had dropped a few minutes before. Several passes firing their 20 mm cannons, which fire huge rounds faster than a machine gun, followed. Then they disappeared.

When the flames were nearly out, we moved in closer and opened fire with our 50-caliber machine guns and automatic M-79 grenade launchers, blanketing the target area again. We waited and then got the order to dismount and begin our part of the mission, which was to sweep through and kill anything still alive.

In order, the first, second, and third platoons walked single file with five meters between each guy into the vegetation. The fourth set up their mortars to provide support if needed. I walked behind a large Black guy named Holliman who carried a sixty caliber machine gun like it was a toothpick. I carried two bandoliers of his ammo, forming an "x" across my chest. If we got into contact, I wanted to be as close to him as I could and be sure he had all he needed. I had six grenades on the straps of my two aid bags; three were smoke to mark our position if we needed a dust off (helicopter evacuation of any casualties), and three were fragmentation type.

As we walked, we tried to put our feet in the preceding guy's footprints. Booby traps were the main weapon of the VC in this area and caused 80 percent of the 9th Division's casualties. They hid them; we found them. It was like playing hide-and-go-seek for all the marbles. To win, you had to keep staring at the ground, but then you could lose the other game, spot-the-ambush.

The heat and humidity were climbing. The oily smell of napalm hung in the air. There was no sound other than that made by our footsteps, kind of a crunching slosh. Everything I was wearing and carrying got heavier. It got harder to keep up with the guy five meters ahead. If I lost him, we'd be in deep shit. I was getting less attentive. I was missing footprints.

The silence was shattered by an explosion then screaming.

"Medic, medic, Doc - I'm hit, Doc, oh God!"

I broke into a sprint in the direction of the sounds without regard to where my feet landed or what I was running through. The jungle opened up, and I could see the wounded guy on the ground calling out about forty yards away if I went straight across the clearing. I bounded over mounds of land that almost fit my stride. I had to be careful; there were holes in these things.

Johnson and I arrived simultaneously. It was Marx. His hometown was next to mine. Word had introduced us yesterday. He had stepped on a booby trap - one small enough to not blow his legs off but big enough to mangle a foot and ankle. He was down, white as a sheet, propped up on one elbow, his eyes wide and terror-filled as he looked down at his wounds and cried out for help. We used big scissors to cut his pants and expose the bleeding tears and gaps in his lower right leg, ankle and foot. We tightened dressings over the wounds to stop or at least slow the bleeding.

Johnson called for a dust off, and he must have given Marx a shot of morphine, because he was settling down. Two guys came with a stretcher, loaded him, put his helmet over his exposed genitals, and carried him to the where the tracks were. A helicopter came and got him.

"Your first dust off, Doc - nice work," Johnson said as we got our gear back together.

"You did all the work," I answered. "I don't know what I would have done without you here."

"It comes with practice, and you'll get plenty. You'll be fine. You did the most important part; you got to him fast."

"Thanks."

"I would make one suggestion, though. Next time, run along the column. Those mounds you were jumping over were a bunker complex. If they'd been in there, you wouldn't be talking to me."

"Is that what that was? No shit?"

"Yeah, so try not to blaze any new trails, okay? We need you."

Later that day, as the third platoon's three tracks cleared the edge of a wood line and roared into the open, terrified people scattered and tried to run into a cluster of four or five hootches, everybody but one. Even as three squads of us jumped off and ran up yelling and waving our M-16's back and forth at them, he never moved. My squad leader, Danny, grabbed him by the front of his black shirt and backed him up against the nearest wall.

"Doc, over here," he shouted. "Cover this guy and if he moves kill him."

The year-long transition from being Walter and Marie's son studying pre-med at Michigan State, to "Doc", the third platoon's medic, was now complete. I had only been in-country about ten days. I had never killed anybody; God gave a commandment against that, but He was not here. Danny Fogle was, and he had just given me an order that I was trained and ready to carry out.

The man at the end of my rifle was a freak. Not only was he a head taller than me, he had blue eyes. From his scarred, expressionless face hung a graying beard composed of about fifteen eight-inch-long hairs. After his people were out of sight, he slowly turned and looked down at me. He supported himself with a wooden staff. I risked a split second glance downward and saw two normal appearing legs and feet. Nothing about him was right or reassuring. He didn't need to make a sound or move; his face said it all: I hate you, and somehow I will kill all of you. A chill passed through my entire body.

"Harkness, Northwood, Holliman, take some men and check out

those other hootches and get 'em all out here." Danny barked. Without alarm or urgency, almost like he knew what was going to happen next, my guy turned his head to watch them. I moved the tip of my rifle from his chest to his left cheek and turned his head back to face forward. This was all wrong. This guy had no business being here. He should have been off somewhere fighting for one side or the other. Either we had walked into an ambush, or, any number of the hootches our guys were going into were booby-trapped. If so, this one would not live to see any of them fall. Then I'd go help whoever I could.

They were taking too long to come out; something was about to happen. Maybe I should kill this guy now so I could be ready for whatever was coming. No, that was not what Danny said; I would have to let him make the first move and then react, hopefully in time. He was unarmed, backed up against the wall of his home, watching his people being attacked. Was that all, or had he mastered being in war and controlling his emotions, actions, and even expression while he waited for the charges he had rigged to be tripped and tear us apart.

What-the-fuck were they doing in there? Any second, one of our people could pick up or move something and this whole goddamn place could blow up. Death was in the air; you could feel it as clearly as the heat and humidity.

Finally, old men, old women, and little kids started coming out of the hootches ahead of our guys. More tracks pulled in and our company commander appeared with Mike, our Vietnamese interpreter. They came over with Danny and the three of them grabbed my guy by his arms, took him about ten yards away and started interrogating him. Danny and Mike got loud on him, and then Mike slapped him up beside the head a few times. Then they got quieter. After a few minutes, they walked him back over to the rest of us.

"Let's move out." The captain said.

I couldn't believe my ears.

"Sir, this guy is all kinds of bad news. I just *know* it."

"He's a wounded ARVN (Army of the Republic of Vietnam), Doc.

Mike says he's okay. He knows this shit better than we do. Let it go."

I couldn't take my eyes off him. I didn't want to turn my back to him. I may have been an FNG, but I had learned to trust my gut.

"Move out, Doc. *Now!*"

Before I headed for the track, I took one last look at the guy's bizarre face which now bore something between a shit-eating grin and a smile. He'd won this round; he knew it. This was not over; I knew that.

I had come to Vietnam with an understanding and acceptance of why this war was being fought, but now, face-to-face with the people themselves, I was uncertain of the most fundamental issue of all: who was the enemy?

A few days later, we were part of a combined operation with an ARVN unit. They were sweeping, and we were the blocking force to intercept any VC pushed our way. I assumed that I was supposed to go with my squad, so I was putting on my aid bags when Danny Fogle walked up.

"We won't need you, Doc."

"Why not?"

"We ain't going to have any contact."

"How do you know?"

"Because operations involving the ARVN's are just photo ops for the 6:30 news back home to show the unity between the two armies saving the world from Communism. The VC knows the ARVN's don't want to get their uniforms dirty trying to flush them out. Take a break."

It was okay with me; I was exhausted. We were in a dry paddy. I spread my poncho liner on the ground between the track and a dike, laid down, and fell asleep. About twenty minutes later, I heard the unmistakable "crack" of an AK-47, followed by a brief volley of fire from M-16's and M-60's. Then there was silence. Since no rounds had created that tearing-through-the-air sound around me, and nobody was yelling "Medic", I went back to sleep. When our guys started coming out of the wood line talking loud and laughing, I woke up.

"We waxed four gooks," one of them announced as they got back to the tracks.

"Hey, Doc, you were dead right about that tall, ugly, blue-eyed fucker from the other day."

CHAPTER 3

As we sat on top of our track riding to wherever it was we were told to go, I looked around at the guys in my squad. We were young men growing up free in America because when the time came, every generation before us had paid the price for freedom. When America entered World War II, my father and uncles enlisted and went overseas. My mother was pregnant with my older brother when he left. When the war ended, the men came home, replaced their wives in the workforce, and fathered more children. Nobody talked about the war, but there were reminders stored away that my brother and I would find and play with: some army uniforms, a parachute canopy, and some medals. There were pictures: of my father and uncles in foreign countries, of my aunts and their infants waiting and hoping for their husbands to come home alive, and of headstones of friends who did not. The price of peace had always been war; it was our turn to make a payment.

We stopped, dismounted, and were humping again. The terrain alternated: wood line, waist deep water, wood line, stream. I hated being in water: there were no safe footprints to follow, cover was limited, and it took a lot less time to get exhausted. Before long I found myself struggling just to keep up and not break the column.

In the short space that I could see ahead, the route was making a jog to the right around what looked like a large mound of dry land. When I reached it, I remembered what Johnson said about not blazing new trails, but this looked safe. I figured I could save fifteen steps by cutting across. I had to go for it. After the first few steps, it looked like a good idea, but then the ground began to get a little soft, then softer, then I was in mud up to my waist. Not only that, I looked up, and the vegetation that had given us an element of cover was gone. I was looking across ten meters of river at a solid wall of jungle.

I tried going faster, but with each step I sunk deeper. By the time I reached the middle of the mound, I was chest-deep in stinking mud, exhausted, and completely exposed. There could have been any number of Vietcong hidden in the wood line across what now looked more like a narrow stream than a river, and there I was, like a torso target on a firing range.

Every ten seconds or so, another grunt would slosh by on the original route and offer a suggestion in hushed tones.

"Jesus Christ, Doc, you'd better get out of that shit."

Then there'd be another.

"Lie on your belly, Doc, and crawl out. You can do it."

A few I didn't recognize were less helpful.

"You're going to slow us down, asshole."

Another shook his head and muttered "goddamn FNG" as he sloshed on by.

It wasn't long before my strength was gone and I couldn't struggle anymore. I could feel eyes on me. I was in the sights of somebody's AK-47, that much I knew. All he had to do was squeeze the trigger. I just hoped he was aiming at my head and was a good shot.

It seemed like forever. Maybe they were just getting their newest guy to give him a confidence builder. In desperation, I got an idea. I leaned forward and set my elbows down on the surface of the mud and sighted down my rifle barrel at the vegetation across the water. Maybe I could make whoever was out there believe I had spotted them, and that I was just taking up a firing position before we all would open up. Then I realized no one had gone by for about a minute. Oh, my God, I thought to myself. I was living my worst nightmare: I'd been left behind.

I couldn't yell or fire a round; that would give away our position. I started clawing at the mud to get free, but it was no use. It was over, and progressively uglier scenarios flashed through my brain, beginning with being captured. A sudden tremendous thud shook the mound like Jello. I jerked my head around. At the other end of a long, log-like piece of wood that I could reach with my arms was Bill Word. I don't know where he found it or how he managed to get it here, but there it was.

"Crawl out onto this, Doc."

I wrapped my arms around and tried to pull myself onto it. It was no use, the mud refused to ease its grip. Word lay down on the other end of the log, crawled out to me, and grabbed the back of my shirt.

"Pull with your arms, Doc. Pull hard."

He did the same. He was a small guy, but right then he seemed to have the strength of a gorilla.

With a loud sucking sound, my body pulled free. I crawled down the log and stood up on solid ground.

"You okay, Doc?" Word asked.

"Yeah. Thanks, Bill."

We were bent over trying to catch our breath.

"Come on, Doc, we gotta catch up."

We rejoined the column. I was scared, embarrassed, exhausted, and now eighty percent covered with stinking mud that added about twenty more pounds. I began to wonder how bad it could be to be dead. Finally, we headed out of the wood line into a clear area and took a break. There were a few bomb craters partially filled with water that guys were jumping into to cool off. I eased in because these were sometimes booby-trapped and washed off the mud.

I sat on the ground and unbloused my pant legs to let the water run out. I saw what I thought were leeches, but on closer inspection, they were fancy-tailed guppies. I used to pay $2.75 a pair for them at Marion's Aquarium back home. I thought about how I used to try to have everything in the tank just right for them: temperature, gravel, lights, and plants. Now they were living in my pants.

We were done for the day, but not for the night. We would be staying out on a night ambush. The company support people came out with a hot meal and told us that Marx was going to make it. A cheer went up.

After dinner, some guys slept, some wrote letters or read some that the support people had just delivered. I was busy talking with Fogle and a couple other guys who wanted to know how I managed to survive running through a bunker complex and how I got out of the mud hole. It was good to hear some laughter, even if it was directed at me.

Even a can of warm Pabst tasted better than our water. I downed it and looked around at my fellow soldiers, the majority of whom were draftees. These guys had been at this for months. I wondered how they coped. The smell of marijuana in the air provided part of the answer. Whatever worked - I didn't care.

I opened up one of my two aid bags to take inventory, and on top was a large plastic bag full of weed. I looked over at Johnson who was holding his breath then nodded his head a couple times as he exhaled.

"We keep it in the aid bags because it stays dry. If you're not okay with it, I'll carry your platoon's with me," Johnson said. "We don't let anybody get too fucked up with it."

"No, it's okay. I just wasn't expecting to find it in here," I answered.

"Help yourself, if you want. You need paper?"

"I'll take a pass."

Johnson was good. I had seen for myself, and others had told me, too. Not only had his skills saved a lot of guys, but he was lucky. Not long ago, he had walked up on a VC in the brush who leveled an AK-47 at Johnson's head and pulled the trigger. The gun jammed, giving Johnson time to pull out his 45-caliber pistol and empty it into the guy.

As the sun was setting, we rode a couple kilometers then walked single file for another one. By the time we stopped, I could hardly see the guy in front of me without bending over to silhouette him against the darkening sky. We deployed Claymore mines and trip flares around our perimeter, established the thirty minute watch rotation, and now it was time to wait in complete silence for the VC to stumble onto our position.

By this time, it was so dark I couldn't tell if my eyes were open or closed. There was no moon, and clouds obscured the stars. This wasn't just darkness; it was the total absence of light. I had not yet slept when it was my turn to be on watch, and the previous guy handed me the starlight scope. In theory, this device was supposed to turn any source of heat, even photosynthesis in the plants, into light. Reality was that at the interface of ground and sky, where people would be moving, it created a heat wave-like distortion. Were it not for an imbedded luminous dial clock to tell you when your thirty-minute watch was over, it would have been worthless.

Even though I was exhausted, I didn't sleep all night, on-watch or off. They knew we were here, and we were sitting ducks. My right index finger stayed on the trigger and my thumb on the safety of my rifle. It started to rain, monsoon-style. It fell so hard it hurt, and it started to accumulate in what had been a dry paddy. Either our intelligence was wrong, or the VC were getting too big a kick out of this to spoil things with an attack. We didn't hear from them.

When morning came, we rolled back into Rach Kien, showered, changed clothes, cleaned weapons, and slept. Later in the afternoon, we had a change-of-command party for the old CO who was leaving and to welcome the new one who was coming on board. It was a big deal. Good leadership was the difference between death and survival. This outfit had been through a lot with the old CO, and he had earned their respect. Nobody knew the new one.

They served us barbecued steaks and shrimp. I thought the steaks tasted a little funny, so I ate about twenty shrimp. At 0430, I was doubled over with severe abdominal cramps and hobbled to the latrine, where it seemed like every morsel of food I had ever eaten was in a race to see who get out of my mouth or ass first. When sick call opened at 0900, thirty-five guys were treated for food poisoning. As a very busy corpsman was putting an injection into each buttock, I told him I knew the steak was bad.

When he finished, he answered, "It was the shrimp."

I was lying on pile of old clothes and flak jackets in a Quonset hut when Fogle walked up.

"How are you feeling?" he asked.

"Fucked," I answered.

"Well get yourself un-fucked. We got a mounted ambush patrol at 1900," he said as he walked away. There was no sense asking if he was kidding; he didn't do that.

"Can we bring a portajohn?" I shouted after him.

When we pulled out that evening, I was sure that the only courageous thing I would be able to do that night would be to accept the risk and hope it was a fart.

At dusk, we headed out for a mounted night ambush, meaning the tracks stayed with us. When we got to where we were supposed to be, it was nearly dark. We made what we could of a circle with three tracks. Before dismounting, I did my best to memorize our surroundings while I could still see them. Woods to my right reaching to Hanoi, a shed about one hundred yards out in a paddy in front, a hooch with a corral with a water buffalo in it to the left, and next to the hooch was a raised up, walled-in family graveyard common in the Mekong Delta. I climbed off the track and was laying out my poncho liner when I heard Holliman whisper just loud enough to be heard.

"Get down and look over there."

I couldn't see anything, and neither could anybody else.

"Out there," Holliman pointed. "Someone's out there."

"I see him," somebody whispered back.

Several M-16's came to eye-level, bodies crouched, and fingers curled around triggers. Eyes alternately blinked and widened to make sure before firing and announcing our position to the whole Mekong Delta.

"Fuck the ambush," Holliman said. "There's a VC out there, and if he gets whatever he's got zeroed in and fires first, some of us are dead."

His finger started the death squeeze.

"Hold it," somebody shouted. "That's Jeffries. He's takin' a shit."

Everybody stood down, and a few laughed. Holliman was not one of them. When Jeffries got back to us, Holliman lit into him.

"Goddamnit, Jeffries, you 'bout went home in a body bag with a yard of shit paper hangin' out your ass. You damn sure best tell more people what the fuck you're doin' next time!"

About fifteen minutes later, I remembered something I needed off the track and went to get it. As I climbed back down, I turned and was facing near where Jeffries had been. A spray of sparks outlined two guys in those flat straw hats kneeling close together. I heard a whooshing sound and felt a breeze go over my head and barely clear the top of the track.

"GET DOWN, DOC!" somebody yelled, and immediately everybody opened fire. When we stopped shooting, I learned that an RPG (rocket-propelled grenade) had just come within three feet from removing my head and blowing up the track. There was a buzz of radio communication, and the plan was to hold this position. We had found what we were looking for.

It was quiet for about two hours. Then I was awakened by a muffled pop, followed immediately by the cry "incoming!"

The mortar round hit ten yards away and metal fragments sheared off the side of one of the tracks.

"Medic, Medic, I'm hit, Medic!" somebody was screaming.

We opened up with everything as before.

I couldn't see a thing so I just ran in the direction of the screams and found the wounded guy, who was between me and where the round landed.

"Where ya hit?" I yelled.

"My fucking leg, Doc, my fucking leg! Oh God, please help me, Doc."

"Which fucking leg?"

It was Darby, another Michigan guy. He had been sleeping on a stretcher on the ground next to his track. Before he could answer, another mortar round hit near us. I grabbed the head end of the stretcher and started dragging it. I stayed on my knees and kept as low as I could. Bob weighed over two-hundred pounds. Progress was about one foot per pull. A third round came in close to us. I couldn't pull any more, but it didn't matter. They had us zeroed in, and the next round would probably kill us both. He was already hit; I was still intact. I covered the side of Bob's body toward the rounds with my body.

When no more fell, I got off him, felt his legs, and found a warm, wet, rip in his left thigh. He screamed in pain and was bleeding heavily. I got my biggest dressing out from under the bag of weed, wrapped it around the site, and tied it down as hard as I could. Bob screamed. I held my hand on it, and it was staying dry.

"Doc, the CO's on the horn; wants to know what we got," somebody said.

I went over to the guy with the radio.

"Frag wound left thigh with heavy bleeding. He's gotta go."

"You're the man on the ground, Doc. You say he goes, he's gone. I'll call the chopper."

"Roger that, 1-6."

I went back to Bob and the dressing was wet. I tightly wrapped two more over it. Bob responded as before. After a few minutes, the new dressings were staying dry.

"Doc, am I gonna lose my leg?"

I felt south of the wound and found no other damage and he didn't scream.

"Move your foot up and down."

He did.

"Chopper's on its way. You'll be roller skating down your driveway in six weeks."

I did not know that, but I knew we were both alive, and I was glad the rounds stopped falling when they did. Reassurance, even if it was bullshit, wouldn't hurt him any. He settled down.

The CO was back on the radio.

"The chopper's almost here, Doc. Guide him in."

"Ah, okay."

I asked one of the guys how to guide in a chopper.

"There's a strobe light in the track for that."

He got it and handed it to me. I climbed on top of the track, turned it on, and held it over my head.

The guys on the ground looked up.

"Doc, what the fuck are you doin'?" You look like the goddamn Statue of Liberty. Get the fuck off of there and put the strobe out in the paddy where the chopper can land before you get your head blown off."

What did I know? I was an FNG.

I did as I was instructed and went back to Bob. The chopper could be heard now.

"You okay?" I asked after I felt the dry dressing.

"I think so. Doc, thanks for what you did."

"You need to lose weight," I told him.

The chopper touched down for just a moment, and as two guys lifted the stretcher, Bob shouted over the noise.

"DOC, MY DRIVEWAY'S GRAVEL."

Things settled down, and once again, it was decided that we would hold our position. A short while later, new rounds came in, and we opened up without a specific target. When we stopped firing, none of us had been hit, but a woman in the nearby hooch was screaming. She repeated two short phrases over and over in Vietnamese. Mike was with us; I asked him what she was saying.

"She say, 'help me, I dying'," he answered.

As it continued, the lieutenant, platoon sergeant, squad leader, and interpreter huddled up. They concluded this could be a trap. We'd been mortared three times; she was probably a VC sympathizer, and her own would take care of her. It was tough to accept, but they knew this war better than me. I had to listen to her and not do what medics are supposed to do.

On-and-on it went, the same out-of-her-head yell of the same words over and over again. The air was heavy with moisture, smoke, and the smell of gunpowder. It kept her screams close to the ground, making them louder and clearer. After a while, I couldn't stand it anymore.

"Danny, I volunteer to go help her. I have morphine and dressings."

"No! You die, we got no medic."

"Then let's blow the goddamn hooch away and finish her off."

"Let it alone, Doc. It's hard for all of us."

As dark as it was, I could still see Fogle's eyes and his big handlebar mustache set firm over his lower lip. I wouldn't question him again on this or anything else he made his mind up on. It was that kind of look on that kind of face.

The screams slowly got less loud and less frequent but more labored. Then they stopped, and there was complete silence.

When the order came, we mounted up and drove off into the darkness.

CHAPTER 4

It was barely dawn. I stood up, stretched, got down on my knees to fold up my poncho liner, and then I froze and stared at it like I had never seen it before. I had a thought so clear and powerful that I actually looked around to see if someone had spoken to me, but there was no one near. I knew without any doubt that this would be the last time that I would fold this thing up. I looked around again; everything going on was as normal as it ever got. I wanted to say something to somebody to chase the thought from my brain, but no one was close enough. Finally, I stood up. It didn't take Einstein to figure out what it meant: today was the day. I didn't know how it would happen, or how bad it would be, but it would be today.

We'd been in and out of chest-deep canals all day; I had a problem getting out of one of them. I splashed around at the edge of it until Bill Word appeared and pushed some palm branches down to me so I could pull myself up the muddy bank.

"Sorry, Bill. Thanks again."

"Don't worry, Doc; we all went through this when we first got here."

We moved out to catch up. The column had stopped because at the head of it, Harkness had just found another booby trap - a grenade with a trip wire. We waited for him to rig some C-4 near it to blow it up. He walked point every day; he didn't trust anyone else to do it.

"FIRE IN THE HOLE!" he yelled when it was ready to detonate.

We all got down on the ground as the C-4 blew up the grenade without injury to anyone.

The day Word introduced us, Harkness told me that his biggest fear growing up was that there would not be a war going on when he got old enough to be in it. It wasn't like he was crazy, and it wasn't just talk; he loved war and being at the heart of it. One day, I asked him how he spotted booby traps, and he told me that the VC marked them in various ways to protect their own. One day, it would be empty mackerel cans, another day, it was something else. He found patterns like that.

After he disposed of this one, the order was spread to take a break. That was good news, but in the process, we bunched up, and that was bad. I was standing next to Larry Cabbott, a big strong kid from somewhere between Phoenix and Tucson. We saw a knife blade and a square piece of canvas on the ground. We knew better than to touch them. Besides that, we were too tired to bend over. We called our platoon leader, Lieutenant Feldon, over to show him. He left Word's side to come and see what we had found.

"Yeah, they're in here all right," he said as he looked down at it.

"Roger that," Larry answered.

I kept looking down. I didn't see anything to suggest this stuff was attached to anything and serving as a trigger. Then it struck me, it was a marker, but was it for the one Harkness just blew up or could there be -

Before I could open my mouth, there was a clear, metallic "click" across the clearing. There was just enough time after his foot hit the trip wire for Word to say, "Oh, no," in a tone more like resignation than fear.

Larry and I jerked simultaneously toward his voice. The force of the blast doubled me over and drove the air out of my lungs. When I hit the ground, both hands went up to cover what felt like a rip in my right upper belly. My left thigh and arm felt huge. Air continued to only go out of my mouth accompanied by a high-pitched groan. All I could hear was a steady sound like trumpets blaring in the center of my head. All I saw was the sky. My first thought was of my mother; this would kill her, too. In my mind, I said a prayer asking God to go easy on me.

Over the blaring horns, I began to hear what sounded like people yelling words I could not make out. They sounded far away at first and then got louder. Oh my God, I thought, we're being overrun. My rifle was gone.

I hoped I would die before having to watch somebody kill me.

The air stopped going out, and I was able to get in short gasps of air if I stayed still. The horns started to subside; the voices were yelling in English. My buddies were screaming for me to help them.

"MEDIC! MEDIC! HELP ME, DOC! I'M HIT! I'M HIT. DOC, HELP ME!"

When I started to get up, I couldn't breathe again, and when I moved my hands, I thought I was feeling guts coming out from underneath them. I fell back down.

As the blaring sound diminished, the screams got still louder and clearer. I could recognize some of the voices: Larry, Lt. Feldon, the new captain. This was a major cluster fuck. When I tried again to move, but I couldn't get air in and started fading out. There was nothing I could do but lie there and listen to the wounded screaming for me to help them, to do my job.

A guy appeared over me, and I squinted in the sun. It was Jeffries. I was relieved to see that someone was still standing. Then he said "oh, shit," and ran off. When he came back, he had Johnson with him. Johnson dropped to his knees and put something under my head.

"Where you hit, Doc?"

"My belly, under my hands," was all I could get out.

"Just hold them there and don't try to move. You're pretty fucked up."

"What was it?" I managed to get out.

"It had to be at least a 105 round to get seven people. It was in a tree with a trip wire across the trail. I'll be back."

Jeffries stayed.

"Help me get up," I said to him.

"Doc, no, you better not. It's not good."

When I tried, I got dizzy and couldn't breathe again. In short bursts of words, I told him, "Take my aid bags, and go put dressings on anybody bleeding. I can't do shit, but you can."

I eased off the pressure I was holding against by belly just enough for him to slide the straps under my hand and go.

A few minutes later, two guys came running up with a stretcher, loaded me onto it, and carried me away. I was conscious, and I could breathe if I lay perfectly still on my back. The sunlight was blinding, and I could not make out who was carrying me. Then they lowered the stretcher to the ground.

"Stay with Doc; I'll go back get somebody else," the guy at the foot end said as he turned and ran back to where we had been.

The other one came over and stood at my right side. He crouched slightly as he swept his M-16 moving back and forth across the nearby woodline.

"I got ya, Doc. I'm here for ya."

I squinted into the sun, and he moved to block it. It was Homey. I remembered just before we pulled out of Rach Kien, he had stopped me.

"I hurt my back, Doc. I can't go. Tell my squad leader you think I have to stay behind, you have the authority to do that."

Johnson had been nearby and overheard him. Homey had asked him first.

"Goddamnit, I already told you we're gonna need every swingin' dick we got including yours on this operation."

"But, Doc Johnson, I'm short, please. I got a bad feeling about this one," he had pleaded.

"Move out, Homey, and don't pull this shit again."

It was quiet now.

"You had it right, Homes; you knew," I said to him.

"Don't try to talk, Doc. This may not be over."

"I'm sorry I-"

"It's okay, Doc, just hang on."

I could hear the chopper in the distance, and Johnson giving instructions to grunts doing their best to be medics. Then I heard him say two words I would never forget.

"Word's dying..."

CHAPTER 5

The flight to Saigon took about twenty minutes. We were loaded into a big green Army ambulance for the trip to the hospital. En route, I looked somewhere other than straight up for the first time. Holliman was on a stretcher across the center aisle. His face was streaked with blood, and his nose was ripped open up the right side, the exposed pink tissue in stark contrast to his jet-black skin. I wanted to look away, but I had caught his eye.

"You're gonna be okay Holliman; that'll go back together fine," I told him.

"Thanks, Doc. You okay?"

"Yeah, I'm okay," I answered.

"Good." He smiled, and it made his wounds gape a little more. I turned and kept my gaze above me for the rest of the ride. Blood had been dripping through the stretcher above me onto my chest since we were put on the chopper. I did not know whose it was. On the ride in the ambulance, it slowed down and then stopped.

After about a fifteen minute ride, we came to a stop then backed up a short ways. The doors swung open, and somebody got in and surveyed the load. He turned back to the door and told two others outside, "we got one for you guys." They were from the morgue. Johnson was right; Word was dead.

We were taken to a triage area where we were engulfed by medical personnel. I told them what I thought I had under my hands.

"You're at Third Field Hospital - go ahead and move them."

I did but there was nothing there. They cut away my clothes. The pain in my belly was referred from a hole in my right chest under my arm. They sat me up. The horns started to blare in my head again, and I started fading out. I felt something like a garden hose get pushed up into my chest, and when they laid me back down, the stretcher was deep with thick, warm blood. They looked at my left arm, which had a metal fragment sticking out of it. There was another in my upper inner left thigh. They read my mind.

"The family jewels are intact," a voice said. Before I could savor the news, someone pushed a rubber tube up my dick. I was too relieved for them to have a place to shove it to be bothered very much by how it felt.

X-rays showed the metal fragment that entered my chest was just above or just inside my liver. There was talk of going to surgery right then, but they decided to wait and watch for a while. They gave me a shot, and I fell asleep.

I don't know how long it was before I became aware of someone standing at the side of my bed and opened my eyes.

"I saw your name when you checked in, Rich, but I didn't want to disturb you. Just couldn't stay out of this thing, huh?"

Gary Jones hadn't changed a bit since AIT.

"Am I dreaming?" was all I could say.

"I been right here the whole time; never went to the boonies at all. In four days, I'm going home."

"Great, I'm glad for you. I felt so bad when you-"

"I remember. I appreciated it, too. Did your friend with the broken neck make it?"

"Yeah, he just finished rehab and is doing pretty good."

"I'm glad. That was pretty rough. This ain't exactly what we had in mind for getting' together again is it?"

"No, it's pretty bizarre. We traded places after all."

"Anything you need just let me know. You're safe now. You're gonna be alright. Get some rest."

Later that night, they put a Black guy in the bed across the aisle from me. His right leg was in a full-length cast, his left leg, his head, and his belly were bandaged and he was out of it. After no one was around, he started moaning and tried to get out of bed. With a chest tube in me, I couldn't call out very loud, but a corpsman finally heard me, and he and a nurse ran over. She kept calling his name.

"Harrison, Harrison, you've got to stay in bed. Benjamin, can you hear me? You can't get up right now."

He slumped back down, and after a long, low moan went into cardiac arrest. While five or six people worked on him, all I could do was fold my and hands and pray that there would be no more death today.

They brought him back, but two hours later, he arrested again, and they could not save him. One of the nurses came over and talked to me. Basically, he'd been blown apart, and they had operated on him all day. He really didn't have a chance.

They took him away and made the bed.

I opened my eyes, and a distinguished looking middle-aged man in starched fatigues was attaching something to the left side of my pillow.

"How are you feeling, Son?" he asked me.

He had a kind face and star on his collar.

"I'm okay, Sir."

"I'm General Gunn, assistant Ninth Division Commander. I've talked to the rest of the guys in your unit. They spoke very highly of you, and they're worried about you. You must be a good medic."

He finished pinning something to my pillow and continued.

"It is my highest honor to present you with the Purple Heart, the United States Army's oldest military decoration instituted by George Washington and awarded to soldiers wounded in the line of duty. I'm proud to have you serving in the 9th."

I looked over at it while he shook my hand. I tried several times to say something but couldn't.

"It's okay. Rest easy, soldier."

Thirty minutes later, Lt. Feldon came in pushing Larry Cabbott in a wheelchair in front of him. They both had cuts on their faces and Barry's legs were in dressings. There were more silent feelings shared than words spoken. Their facial expressions reflected the emotional confusion we felt: the relief that we were here and alive and the grief and guilt that a friend was not. They would visit daily until they were sent elsewhere a couple days later.

The next time I woke up, the new CO was standing at the foot of my bed. The empty right sleeve of his pajama top was dangling apathetically at his side. That shoulder was wrapped in a bulky white dressing, and the arm was in a sling.

"How ya doin', Doc?"

His demeanor was totally changed. Seventy-two hours earlier, he'd been standing in a paddy with no shirt yelling into a wood line for Charley to try and kick his ass. I remembered thinking at the time: great, a gung-ho FNG, and he's calling the shots.

"I'm okay. Are you all right?"

"My shoulder's tore up, that's all," he said.

It was quiet for a moment. As an infantry captain, Vietnam was a career opportunity, and his job was to roam around looking for VC in black pajamas. Now he was visiting his own men in blue ones in a hospital. He looked and sounded like he felt responsible for what happened, and I felt sorry for him, but I felt sorrier for Word.

"Get some rest, Doc. I'll check on you later."

"Okay, 1-6" (his number over the field radio.)

My stay at Third Field lasted twelve days, unusually long for that facility. Most got patched up, stabilized and sent either to in-country convalescent centers or back to the States. After my chest tube was taken out, it had to be put back in because blood had re-accumulated. During the period between tubes, I was ambulatory and roamed the facility at will.

The hospital had been a school before the war. Some of the wards had been classrooms, and a huge one had been a gymnasium. One served as a burn unit. The first time I saw a group of young girls whose faces had been burned by napalm, I nearly had to turn away. I focused on their eyes, not the scars. They were just like all kids: shy, silly, energetic. I knew how to say hello and could count to ten in Vietnamese, and I knew the terms for male and female.

That was enough to make me a hit with the napalm girls. What I thought meant sweetheart in Vietnamese actually turned out to mean grandma, which explained why they would crack up every time I said it. When my chest tube had to be put back in, they came to see me every day in ICU. After the second tube was removed, I could roam about the facility again.

The sound of an ambulance siren as they arrived at Third Field was commonplace during my stay. A couple of days before I left, it was almost non-stop for several minutes. I headed down to the triage area to see what was up.

By the time I got there, the area was filling up with casualties, only this time, they weren't mud and blood covered GI's - they were Vietnamese kids. The Vietcong had something called "sapper teams," which operated in small numbers and usually in populated areas. Their main weapon was the "satchel charge," a bag of explosives they could hurl into a building or into crowds to intimidate, terrorize, and, of course, kill. Today, the target was a school bus stopped for a moment on a busy Saigon street. They opened the back door, threw in the bag, and blew the bus and the kids apart.

With sirens blaring, the ambulances brought them here a few at a time until there were about a dozen of them and twice that many medical staff filling the triage area. Each kid filled just over half the length of a gurney; all were cut and bleeding. Those who were conscious were screaming so loud that the medical staff had to shout their instructions to each other. Many kids were unconscious, and their heads and extremities flopped, powerless against gravity when lifted or repositioned. The eyes of the dying stayed open, seeing nothing.

I watched, helpless and horrified, from a covered walkway adjacent to the area. These were innocent kids with parents, siblings, and relatives who loved them dearly, and they were being used as pawns in a sick game played by adults. What possible justification for this could there be? Body counts, collateral damage – it was all utter madness. I was filled with hate for the animals that did this: they deserved to die, and I wanted to kill them. Then I wanted no part of this insanity which killing only perpetuated. I tried to focus on efforts to save these children. Thank God there were still some people on the planet with the knowledge, expertise, and willingness to help put the pieces back together. The medical staff worked like a well-oiled machine and embodied values more fundamentally human and powerful than either side's rationalizations for its actions.

I vowed on the spot that if I made it back home alive, I would try again to become a doctor and try to make a positive difference when bad things happened to people. As for the war, I didn't start it, and I couldn't end it. While it went on, I would do my best to help people survive it, to make a difference. From that moment on, that's all I wanted to do.

My bed was now in the big gym ward at the opposite side of complex from the triage area, and the walk back took longer than usual. Once inside, I passed the bed of a guy I had come to know a bit.

"Big Bear, how ya doin'?"

"That you, Rich?"

Big Bear was a huge man, and his job had been defusing explosive devices. Two big white pads covered where his eyes had been, his face was a network of sutured cuts, and what was left of his hands were in white dressings the size of boxing gloves.

"Yeah, it's me."

"Do you know what the hell all the sirens were about?"

I told him what I just seen.

"Fucking bastards," he snarled.

"You got that right."

"Hey, do you know what time it is?" he asked.

"Yeah, it's 9:30," I answered.

"A.m. or p.m?"

I wished I hadn't made him ask me that.

I made my way down the aisle and laid down on my bunk. I was physically and emotionally drained and fell asleep in seconds.

I heard a voice ask if I wanted a visitor. I opened my eyes.

"Hello, my name is Michael Anthony."

Standing at the side of my bed was actor Marvin Miller who had played that role in the TV show. He was touring Vietnam with the USO. I immediately and uncontrollably broke down.

"I'm sorry, I didn't mean to upset you. I'll go."

"No, no, please, just give me a second. I'll be okay, please."

I took some deep breaths, and I was able to tell him about how Tom and I used to say we were never going to work and just wait him to bring the check. His face beamed and he laughed loudly. I could not stop shaking his hand.

"I have it right here, a check for one million dollars'-worth of good luck from The Bank of Good Will. Just sign here."

"Thank you for coming here. Thank you for doing this. I can't tell you what this means to me," I sputtered as I signed.

"I did this to feel exactly what you made me feel just now," he answered. "*I* thank *you*."

"Wait: could you write one for my friend? He got blown up here last year. He's quadriplegic, but he's doing well. It would mean so much to us."

"Absolutely!"

The day before I left Third Field, I was walking down the main concourse when I heard somebody call to me from one of the wards.

"Hey, Doc, over here."

Everybody from the cluster fuck was long gone at this point. I looked around, and there with his left arm thickly wrapped in a dressing and dangling from an IV pole was Danny Fogle. It took a second to recognize him because he was smiling, and I had never seen him do that.

"Great to see you, Doc! Christ, when you left, I thought you were dead, and then we heard they sent you back to the States."

"What happened, Danny?"

"Oh we walked into a goddamn ambush; machine gun blew my arm to shit. They're gonna give me a new elbow."

He had already tripled the total number of words he had spoken to me since I first met him. He was a different person; the relief of being out of the war and free of command responsibilities lit up his whole face.

"When are you goin' home?" he asked.

"I'm not leaving."

"What?"

"No. I just had a talk with my doctor; I asked to stay. I'm going to 6th Convalescent Center for a month, and then back to the unit."

"*What?*"

"It's a long story. I've seen some shit here that put this whole thing into a new perspective for me."

"Wow."

"Can I get you anything, Danny?"

"No, Doc, but come back after lunch. We're havin' ice cream."

Sixth Convalescent Center at Cam Rahn Bay was on a white sand beach with the blue-green South China Sea in front and purple gray mountains in the distance behind. The sounds of F-4's taking off and landing at their adjacent airbase and the occasional rumble of artillery in the distance were reminders that this was still Vietnam and there was a war going on.

Security was provided by a unit of the South Korean Army. They had a reputation as fierce fighters who sometimes had a problem accepting an enemy combatant's death as an indication to stop inflicting damage. The North Vietnamese and the VC wanted no part of them. I liked that and the fact that another country committed their sons to this effort.

There were about eight-hundred ambulatory patients here: an army of soldiers in blue pajamas without weapons. It was a good place for Darby and I. We ran into each other the day after I arrived. We talked a little about when he got hurt, but we didn't dwell on it. Darby returned to our unit after about a week; I would remain another three weeks.

Our bodies were healing, but none of us knew there was a psychological component to our experiences that would leave us permanently changed and produce varying degrees of consequences in our lives from then on. For me, the earliest indications of that began to appear here.

I was in the library one day reading the Army newspaper, The Stars and Stripes. It was published daily, and once-a-week it listed the names of those killed in action the week before. I stopped reading at: "Freeman, Robert. Specialist fourth class, Ypsilanti, Michigan. KIA."

Freeman had been part of my other life. We had lived on the same floor at Michigan State. We studied, partied, cheered for the Spartans, played cards, and laughed a lot. After that, we went our separate ways, but I knew he was out there somewhere. Maybe we would run into each other at an MSU game someday. Now, he was no more than a line in a newspaper saying his life was over. It ended here. He wouldn't live a long life and die of natural causes; he was killed, here. This was as close to our paths crossing as we would get. I didn't know whether to grieve or be angry.

A couple of days later, Life Magazine put out an edition showing the photos taken at the start of basic training of the 248 soldiers killed in action in Vietnam in one particular week - the week of the cluster fuck, to be exact.

I was looking at a 1/125th second shutter snap of what had been a life. The soldiers were dead, but the pictures lived and were still communicating something about that person. Did the ones with the serious expression have a premonition of their death? Were the others smiling to mask fear, or were they resigned to whatever was about to happen? What were they trying to tell me?

Also, neither Bill Word nor Benjamin Harrison was included. Did somebody forget to report them, or, worse yet, purposely omit them? Could there be others left out of that week, other weeks, every week? Was our KIA data as phony as what we pegged on the enemy?

I stared at them until lights out.

Then, I didn't know if I was asleep and dreaming or still awake and thinking, but I was seeing the photos I had received in the mail earlier that day from the reunion in New Jersey. In every one, my face appeared as an unprinted negative.

In the morning, I avoided looking at faces or making eye contact with anyone. I decided that either I had lost my mind, or I was about to. That is not something you want to tell just anybody. In the Army, you go to the chaplain.

His place was between my ward and the mess hall, and I walked past it half-a-dozen times a day, never feeling any need to avail myself of his services until now. I did not know or care about his denomination. I just needed a neutral party to hear what was going on in my head before it got any worse. I knocked, and the door opened.

"Chaplain, could I talk to you? I'm having a problem."

"Sure, that's why I'm here. Come on in, sit down, and make yourself comfortable."

It was a nice, apartment-like place with a couple of easy chairs. It had the look and feel of home.

"Coffee?"

"Okay, thanks."

He poured us each a cup, brought them over, and sat down across from me. We did a little more introducing.

"Okay, Rich. How can I help you?"

He made me feel comfortable enough to spill my guts. I told him everything from folding the poncho liner to what I experienced yesterday. Then there was silence.

"So, basically, what you're telling me is that you've had a crash course in war."

I thought about it. In just that single sentence, he took everything that was so ill-defined and overwhelming for me and put it into a perspective I had not considered.

"Yeah. You're right. I'm not crazy; the war is."

I could have left right then and done better, but he wasn't done.

"War forces us to experience unimaginably horrible events and feelings. I think at the heart of it for you was a very unfortunate coincidence. What I will call your 'poncho premonition' was a thought - a very powerful one - which happened to be followed by an event - a very powerful one. The one did not cause or forecast the other. They just happened close together."

I looked up at his face.

"You are going to continue to experience feelings as strong or maybe even stronger, after which, nothing is going to happen. After you see that a few times, you'll deal better with anything that does happen. You're not losing your mind; you're using it, maybe too much, but it is understandable."

He sounded more like a shrink than a sky pilot. Not once did he say anything about God's plan for me or tell me to read the Bible. I liked that a lot. My faith stopped working for me, or vice versa, the day that I attended mass in an open wood-frame shelter with an M-16 in my hands. The priest performed the same ceremony and wrapped it up with the same "the mass is ended, go in peace." I just knelt there looking at him. Something was drastically wrong with this picture.

I knew the predominant religion of North Vietnam was Buddhism, but there were many Catholics. Their sons and daughters simultaneously heard this same directive while they were on their knees holding their AK-47's. Shortly, we would both be out there trying to kill each other. I always felt that the church should have had more to say about that. If it had, maybe both sides' Catholics could have just stood up and said, "The war is ended, go to mass," and that would have been the end of the whole Goddamned thing.

We talked a while about other things, and then I thanked him and left. I'd see him out and about and give him a "thumbs-up" and he'd return an "okay" sign. He helped me. I felt a lot better, and he proved to be right, but I would never look at Life magazine again.

I would be leaving 6th Convalescent Center and returning to Bien Phouc in a few days. I was fully recovered and ready. I was lying on the beach when Murphy, a guy from my ward who had been there my entire stay, came up to me.

"The ward sergeant wants to see you," he told me.

"Now?" I asked.

"I don't know. It was kind of strange. He said if I saw you to tell you he wanted to see you when you had a chance."

"Was he pissed?"

"No, he was, I don't know, like concerned maybe?"

I rolled up my bamboo mat, walked back to the ward, and found him.

"Murphy said you wanted to see me, sergeant. What's up?"

"Yeah. How are you feeling?" he asked.

"Good."

"Do you think you're being well cared for?"

"Yeah, it's been great here. Thank you for your help."

"Good. You're welcome. The CO wanted to know, too. Why don't you go over and tell him how you are?"

I thought maybe he had gotten into the Demerol or something. This was weird.

"Sarge, what the fuck is going on?"

"Well, there's been a presidential inquiry into your condition."

I had to let that sink in for moment before responding.

"A what?"

He repeated what he had said.

"What does that mean?"

"Well, why don't you just head down and see the CO, and he can probably explain it better than me."

"You mean now?"

"Yeah, he's expecting you."

I put my pajamas on over my green boxers and headed for the orderly room. During my time in the service, trips to orderly rooms had a mixed track record as to outcomes. I had no idea what to expect this time.

When I arrived, the first sergeant took me right into the CO's office.

"Specialist Czop reporting, Sir," I said as I saluted and stood at attention.

"At ease. Have a seat."

He was relaxed, pleasant, but in command. He was Black.

"How are you coming along?"

"Fine, I expect to be back to my unit next week."

"That's good. Have you received good treatment here?"

"Yeah, I mean, yes, sir, fine, but I'd like to know what this is all about. My sergeant said something about a presidential inquiry into my condition. What does that mean?"

He flipped some papers held together with a paper clip across the desk.

"Read this."

The pages were photocopies of a hand written letter from my mother to Richard M. Nixon, the President of the United States of

America, the Commander-in-Chief of the American Military. It began: Dear "Tricky Dick," and went straight downhill from there. I shook my head as I tossed the papers back onto his desk.

"I'm sorry about this, Sir. My mother is Sicilian, and sometimes she…"

"It's okay. Read the whole thing; I'm in no hurry. It's a good letter."

Certain passages stood out more than others. "If this war is so important, why is your son-in-law hiding out in the White House instead of fighting in it? He's supposed to come from a family of such great Americans… If you were elected, you were supposed to have a plan to end this thing in a few months… "Tricky Dick" sure fits you well… How the hell do you let those people in there and set those booby traps anyway… I want my son out of there, NOW!"

I put it down again and looked up at the CO.

"I'm embarrassed."

"There's nothing embarrassing about a mother loving her son. If the mother of everybody who's over here wrote a letter like this one, we probably wouldn't be in this war."

We talked for a while about wars and mothers and children. As a man in charge of a center of healing in a war zone, I was very interested in everything he had to say. He spoke from the heart. Then we wrapped up.

"I'll take care of the paperwork on this thing. You might want to write and clear up some of your mother's technical misconceptions about how things are set up over here. I've enjoyed talking with you."

"Likewise, Captain, and thank you for everything you're doing."

He got up and walked around the desk. I stood, we shook hands, and he escorted me to the door.

"Good luck, Rich."

There was no salute, dismissed, or other bull shit.

Two days after I returned to my unit, I read in the Stars and Stripes that sapper teams had come out of the South China Sea at night, run up the beach, and thrown satchel charges into several of the wards of 6th Convalescent Center, including the ones on either side of the one I had been in. Ninety-seven already wounded men were wounded again, and three were killed.

CHAPTER 6

"How are ya, Top?" I asked.

"Can I help you?" he answered.

He was sitting at his big impressive desk, shirtless as always. It had been over six weeks since I'd been in the aid station. I had grown a mustache and lost weight while I was away.

"Yeah, I'm back to help you win the war. Spec. 4 Czop, Bravo Company, third platoon medic."

When he recognized me, his face lit up.

"Doc! Jesus Christ! What are you doing here? First we heard you were dead, and then we heard they sent you back to the States! How are you? Damn, it's good to see you."

"Hey, it's damn good to be seen. I'm okay, how about you?"

"I'm great. I'm out of here in a few days. I'm going home. They've started a 25,000 troop pullout. A bunch of the guys are leaving."

"Hey, that's great! I'm happy for you."

"Are you back or just visiting?"

"Are you getting a lot of tourists through here these days, Top?"

He laughed.

"I got a deal for you. I'm going to give you the Medcaps. You ain't humpin' anymore. You've paid your dues. I can't believe they sent you back."

"I asked to come back."

"Are you nuts? You had a million dollar wound. You could have gone home."

"That was only because good people were there to help when we all went down. Maybe I can do that for somebody else. What's Medcaps?"

"It stands for Medical Civic Action Program."

"What do I have to do?"

"Oh you just take this big box of supplies and go to the villages and basically run sick call for the Vietnamese a few days a week. You have your own track and driver, and you take Mike to interpret. It's the easiest thing I can give you. Sound okay?"

"I'll give it a shot. Thanks, Top."

The team consisted of me, Mike, whoever was available that day as track driver, and one of the grunts riding the fifty caliber machine gun. When we couldn't get a grunt, I doubled as medic and machine gunner. The man-in-charge was named Belinski, a staff sergeant from the intelligence section. I didn't like him. Even worse, I didn't trust him. He was gung-ho, and from what I had seen so far, that did not bode well.

The rules of search and clear were simple and straight forward: if they shoot at you, kill them; if they run, kill them; if you're not sure, kill them. For our operation, they were not as precise: if it doesn't feel right, get out fast; don't turn your back on anyone; never let anybody get between you and the track and the fifty cal.

We would go to the center of a village, Mike would announce our purpose over a bullhorn, and people would start peeking out. Then a few would slowly walk up to check us out. Before long, there'd be as many as thirty appreciative South Vietnamese people jammed around us for whatever care we could provide. There was no schedule or pattern to our visits to avoid being ambushed. The VC hated Americans being helpful to the South Vietnamese. Killing us in front of a crowd of them would get some VC a promotion.

Things went well enough until the mission's priorities were changed and greater emphasis was placed on intelligence gathering about VC movements than winning the hearts and minds of the people. Soon, there were no more villages, hamlets, or crowds of kids. We were being sent into remote areas, and the people we encountered were less friendly. Twice we were sent out with two squads of grunts on two tracks providing security, and on one of those, we had to shoot our way out of a bad situation. The next day, a ninety-man company was sent to search and clear that area.

"I don't like it, Belinski."
"Relax, Doc. We'll be in and out in a few minutes."
"That jungle shit is too dense and way too close to that hooch."
"We got our orders, Doc. They want us to check this place out."
Belinski ordered the driver to slowly move up closer to the hooch. If we took fire, he would have his recon info. One of us might be dead, but the mission would have been a success.

An old farmer came out of the hooch and said something friendly.
"See, Doc?" Belinski said.
"Oh, yeah - like he's going to say 'my boys are in the wood line fixin' to blow your asses away.'"

We dismounted, and the four of us walked up, M-16's at our sides, to meet the old man halfway to the hooch. He and Mike talked in Vietnamese. He said they had a sick kid inside. Mike told them I could help him. The old man called into the hooch and the kid came out limping badly on his right foot, which was wrapped in rags. Mike told him lie down, I knelt next to him and everybody else followed the old man into the wood line.

The kid looked about seven-years-old, and he felt warm as I carefully removed the layers of rags from his right foot and exposed an infected wound. He had stepped into a small punji pit, a hole covered with vegetation concealing razor sharp sticks of bamboo embedded in the bottom. The tips were dipped in feces to assure infection. One had gone completely through the foot. I would need some things that I kept in the track.

As I stood and turned, I gasped, raised my M-16, pressed my cheek against the stock, and sighted down the barrel onto the back of his head. Three more strides, and the Vietnamese male who had come out of nowhere would be aboard the track and blowing saucer-sized holes in me with the 50-cal. My right finger wrapped around the trigger. With one squeeze red brain would be splattered all over the side of the green track.

"DUNG LAI (HALT)!" I shouted.

He froze. He bought us both some time. I took a short breath without moving the rifle. I had fucked up.

"LA DAI, (COME HERE)!"

He turned around and faced me from twenty meters away. He couldn't have been any older than sixteen. His eyes were wide and fixed on me. I didn't see a weapon. He made no effort to move.

It was the first time in the war that I sighted down the barrel of my rifle onto a live target in broad daylight. As I studied him, competing maxims flashed through my mind like bolts of lightning: the quick or the dead, men, which are you going to be; thou shalt not kill; he who hesitates lets his buddies die.

"LA DAI!" I yelled louder.

He did not move.

I didn't want to kill him, but I didn't want to die or let my team get killed. I had an M-16 now aimed at the bridge of his nose, but I had a rosary in my pocket and a St. Christopher Medal around my neck. One move, and I would have to do something that would haunt me the rest of my life. If I didn't, the four of us would not have a rest of our lives. I had no idea if he was alone or what might be going on behind me, and I couldn't look, or this guy would be on the track. I had to act; I was running out of time.

I motioned with my rifle for him to move out of my most direct route back to the track. It was his last chance, but he didn't move. I had no choice but to kill him. I had pictured myself in a hundred scenarios where I thought I would have to take a life in this war. In none was it me one-on-one with an unarmed kid in no kind of uniform in the bright sunlight of a beautiful day. I was trained and empowered to do this, to gently squeeze, not pull, the trigger, so as not to deflect the barrel from the target. It was time.

"DOC, NO. DON'T SHOOT HIM. DOC, NO."

Out of the corner of my eye, I saw Belinski and Mike running out of the wood line.

They reached me panting. I had yet to lower my rifle.

"It's okay, Doc, just take the rifle down."

I didn't, but I turned my face to them.

"He's the chief's grandson, he's not right, retarded or blown up or something." Belinski said between breaths.

"We gotta get outa here fast. The old man showed us where the VC has rice and weapons hidden. They're close, and they'll be back."

I had nearly killed a twelve-year-old, brain-damaged child looking for peanut butter from C-rations other GI's had given him in the past.

The next day, a company would sweep the area and take the kid to a hospital.

When I got back to the aid station, everybody was huddled around the TV.

"Now what?" I growled their way.

"Be quiet!" someone answered. "We just landed the first man on the moon."

I stood there, looking more at them than at the TV. We were the new generation to whom the torch had been passed. I pictured something different for this moment when I listened to Kennedy's inaugural address and he committed us to accomplishing the feat by the end of the decade. Now, here was one man representing the culmination of a dream of all men before him, and here we were in a nightmare that kept getting worse. I hung up my M-16 on the hook by the door and walked out of the bunker. I sat down on the empty artillery boxes out front and just stared at the ground.

After a couple of minutes, Bandaid came walking up and sat down in front of me. When I didn't acknowledge him, he put his paw on my knee. He kept doing it until I looked at him and started talking.

"You do know you're fucked don't you, Bandaid?"

He wagged his tail and gave me that smile of his.

"You know some VC is going to eat you when this goddamn thing is over, don't you?"

He whined and wagged his tail harder.

"All you understand is English. You even bark with an American accent."

He put both feet on me and tried to climb on my lap while licking my tears. I put my arms around him and buried my face in his neck.

"Thank you," I sobbed.

If a dog loves you, you can't be all bad.

A couple of hours later, I found Lt. Feldon.

"Can you do me favor, L-T?"

They made him company commander while I was away. We had said hi but hadn't really had a chance to sit and talk until now.

"Name it, Doc."

"I want to come back on line with the company."

"I'm glad, Doc. They're just using you guys for bait. It's not right, and I've told them how I feel about it. I wasn't sure how you felt, though."

"I like my chances with ninety guys around me better."

"I understand, but I have to tell you something first. We ain't walked into a wood line since the day we got blown up. They're pulling twenty-five-thousand troops out. The last GI to die in Vietnam isn't going to be one of mine. You okay with that?"

Feldon was always good; metal fragments made him better.

"That's fine by me."

"I'll take care of the paper work. Welcome back, Doc. I'll put you with the mortar platoon. Your humpin' days are over. We're standin' down for forty-eight hours, then you can head out with us."

"Roger that. Thank you, Sir."

The next morning I was talking to one Bravo Company's other medics. Ernie celebrated the lunar landing by getting drunk and doing a face-first landing into his bunk. He forgot to empty the aid station's piss can, and it over flowed. Top was not happy and had him burning the shit from the latrine. You pulled these sawed off fifty-gallon drums out the trap door in the back of the latrine, added fuel oil, lit it, and stirred for about an hour, and then, no shit.

Ernie was a good medic. He got the Silver Star for his actions helping wounded while under fire. We were talking.

"The joke's on Top. I'd rather be doin' this than the bullshit the company's doin' today. This cures a hangover, too."

I told him I was going back on line and why.

"I don't blame you one bit. Things are black and white on line. I can't stand that fucker Belinski. He was with us for a while. Did you know that?"

"No, I didn't."

"We were close to fraggin' the son of a bitch. That's why he's doin' what he's doin' now."

The clerk from the battalion orderly room was headed our way. As he neared, we could see a big grin on his face.

"Who needs flush toilets when we got you, Ernie?"

"Fuck you," Ernie laughed.

Then the clerk turned to me.

"Doc, you can't go back on line."

"Why not?" I shot back.

I glared at him and loaded up both barrels to fire back at what I thought I was going to hear.

"You're being pulled out and sent to Hawaii."

"What is this, somebody's sick idea of a joke?"

"Nope. Here; read this."

He handed me a few sheets of paper. I quickly scanned them and found my name and read the order. Effective immediately, I was being reassigned to the 9th Aviation Battalion in Dong Tam, which was in the process of deactivating, with the subsequent relocation of their medical personnel to Schoffield Barracks on Oahu, Hawaii.

"Fuck-an-A, Doc, congratulations," Ernie said. "What about me?" he asked the clerk.

He looked down at the burning shit barrels and then up at Ernie's face.

"We can't lose a guy with your skills, Ernie; not right now anyway." Then he turned back to me.

"By the way, you never picked up your ARCOM. Here, take this."

He handed me a green folder and a black box.

"What's this?"

"Open the folder," he said.

I had been awarded the Army Commendation Medal for Valor, for "disregarding his own painful wounds and going to the aid of my fallen comrades."

"But I didn't do that. I tried, but I couldn't."

"Well, somebody saw it differently. Congratulations."

I just shook my head. Nothing was "real" about this or the whole fucking war for that matter.

"I can't accept this."

"I'm not taking it back; I got enough paper work to deal with for this pullout. Take it. You've been through more shit in less time than a lot of guys."

"He's right, Doc. You should have got the Bronze for what you did for Darby. They just got the day wrong. Go pack."

Ernie took off his right glove and shook my hand. How I felt about the medal could not detract from the fact that forces beyond my control were ordering me out of the war. The descent into hell was over.

PART TWO

CHAPTER 7

I came out of the jet way at Detroit Metro Airport, spotted my family, and ran to them. I hugged my mom first and longest, then dad, my brother, and his wife. I had lived with the fear that this moment would never happen since that day at Fort Dix. It almost didn't. It was like being reborn as an adult.

On the ride home, we took no fire, hit no mines, and didn't get stuck in any mud. Once in the driveway, I stood there and looked at our damage-free, unfortified house, and listened for distant sounds of war. There were none. We went in and sat down at the kitchen table; and that's when it struck me: this was real, I was home. We had some lunch and talked awhile, catching up on family and neighborhood news. Near the end of the meal, it was quiet for a moment.

"Rich, it was so hard for me when you got hurt," my mother confessed.

I just listened.

"I have to tell you something, and you're going to think I'm crazy, but when you were wounded, I jumped out of bed in the middle of the night holding my right side. It woke your father, and he asked me what was wrong. 'Richard's been hurt,' I told him. He told me I was just having a bad dream. 'Like hell. Don't die, Rich, please don't die. Don't give up, fight,' I just kept saying over and over."

She was crying; I got up and put an arm around her.

"That wasn't crazy, Ma. When we got blown up, it felt like somebody hit me in the belly with a full swing of a baseball bat. I didn't think I was going to breathe again, and my first thought was what it would do to you if I didn't. I don't know what took place, but something did for sure. 'Don't ever underestimate the power of a mother's love' the commanding officer at the convalescent center told me. I think that's the best explanation."

She held tightly onto my arm. We gathered ourselves, and I changed gears.

"So, Mom, how are you and Nixon getting along these days?"

After lunch, I went over to see Tom. I could have walked, but I hadn't driven a car in five months, and I wanted to get the feel of being back on the block. His house was on a corner, and I parked alongside in the spot where we talked the night before he left for Vietnam. I sat there for a second and watched a car go by. We used to play catch in the street and get out of the way when cars passed. One time, he tagged one of them on the trunk as it went by and in the process, his mitt came off. He kept up with that car for a block before it stopped and he got it back.

I went to the screen door and Tom's brother, Bob, called out before I could knock.

"Come on in, Rich."

It was the first time I was in the house since Tom had been injured, and the first time I had seen the whole family in the living room at the same time without a Christmas tree up. Tom was in his wheelchair. I shook his hand and patted him on the shoulder, then shook hands with his Dad and his two brothers: Bob, four years older, and Don two years older.

"Welcome home, idiot," Tom started right in. "You scared the shit out of everybody. Just exactly what happened to you? It sounded pretty bad,"

"I just had the wind knocked out of me. Now it just hurts to cough or sneeze, and I feel a pull when I walk past large magnets, but otherwise I'm fine. Then my mother told Nixon to bring me home, and here I am."

Everybody laughed.

"Seriously," his mother added, "we're so glad you're back. We could not have taken anything worse happening to you. We've had enough."

After hanging out for a while, I went home and as I drove back, I had the thoughts that would shape how I would deal with my own Vietnam experiences for the next forty-three years. All I did there was come to a better understanding and greater appreciation of what Tom and others who fought during the worst of the war had been through. What happened to me during a few bad months were now just memories in my head, nothing more, and not worth mentioning. Tom was the soldier; he paid a price worse than death. My experiences and wounds were nothing compared to his, so I had no right to feel anything.

There were reasons to be optimistic about the future. The war was winding down. America had honored its commitment as a member of the Southeast Asia Treaty Organization to defend nations in that region if they came under attack by Communist forces. We bought the South Vietnamese time and trained and equipped them to take over the fight. The feeling that enough young American lives had been lost was growing, and I agreed. It was time get out, and we were. The racial issues that had threatened to tear the country apart still existed, but the most significant battles against segregation and discrimination were now being waged in the courts and Congress instead of in the streets of large cities. I was glad because in Vietnam, both Black and White bled red.

On the personal side, I was at Wayne State back in pre-med the day after my discharge, and Tom would soon be attending Western Michigan University across the state in Kalamazoo majoring in psychology. One night I went to watch my old high school's basketball team play a game in the state's regional tournament. I saw a classmate of mine in the stands and sat with him. Jim Brice was in the desk in front of me in Latin class that day in junior year when we learned JFK had been assassinated. He had a good job and was looking for an apartment. So was I and we wound up getting one that was convenient to Wayne State and his work site. We both liked sports, food, and fun. He introduced me to his younger sister, Janine, and we took her out to a bar to celebrate her twenty-first birthday. She was beautiful, fun, and nearly engaged to some guy who was out of town that day. I liked her.

Then the politicians took over. On April 30, 1970, with the words "this is not an invasion of Cambodia," President Richard M. Nixon invaded Cambodia. I thought maybe somebody had made a mistake and handed him a speech from 1968, but that was not the case. American troops had secretly been in Cambodia on his order long before this date, and that information was about to be leaked. Nixon had a thing about leaks and a bad track record with secret plans. The one that got him elected in 1968 was supposed to end the Vietnam War within three months. Whether he never really had one or it just didn't work was academic to all but the 5,000-plus soldiers who were subsequently killed in action, and their families. Taking bold action to cover his tracks in Cambodia and then selling it as effective leadership, helped his chances for re-election but ignited a firestorm.

The backlash on campuses across America was immediate and intense. I expected the inevitable showdown to occur at Berkley or some other large university with a track record of anti-war activism, not Kent State, where three days of rioting prompted Governor James Rhoades to announce: "we are going to eradicate the problem… it's over with in Ohio."

On May 4, 1970, I heard about it on the radio riding home from classes and then watched it on the 6:30 news. The Ohio National Guard opened fire on a crowd of student demonstrators, killing four and wounding ten. There were the screams, the bleeding bodies, the chaos, but now it was not Vietnam, it was Ohio, and it wasn't soldiers. It was a bunch of kids from all over the place who were ten years old when the first Americans appeared in Vietnam. They were protesting against governmental policy. Every soldier since George Washington, including me, fought to assure them of that right.

As I watched them on their bellies and backs dying, all I could think was where does this end? How many more have to die here or over there before we can have something called peace with something called honor? It was time to save *lives* – not face. It was time to stop destroying and start rebuilding, but the Nixon Administration didn't see it that way. The politics of paranoia, hatred, and divisiveness would continue at home, and the politics of bombs and bullets would continue in Southeast Asia.

Consequently, as the first anniversary of the cluster fuck in Vietnam neared, I was having a difficult time. Jim and Janine had an older sister who had died at twenty-one of lupus while we were in high school. Janine found a batch of poems that had helped her and her family work through that tragedy. She could see I was having problems with Vietnam, past and present, and she gave me the poems.

"These might help you. I know the circumstances were very different, but they have losing someone close to you in common. If you want to talk, I'm here."

"Thanks. I appreciate that," I told her.

I read them all, they helped, and because of Janine's thoughtfulness, I decided to cancel my plans to get drunk on May 28, 1970 and opted for something more constructive. I wrote some thoughts about the war and Bill Word on a single page of paper, and one of my professors let me run off a hundred copies on her mimeograph machine. I passed them out on campus that day, but I avoided getting into any conversation with anyone about it.

> "My friend will never know whether you think he was a patriot or a murderer, and no one can speak for him. I just want somebody to know that one year ago today, his light went out, and if you didn't know him, you never will. He'll live in my mind as a symbol of all that's horrid and futile about violence and hatred."

After that, Janine and I started seeing more of each other. I studied, she worked, and we had fun together.

"If you don't stop pacing around, I'm going to roll a wheel on your foot."

I was nervous. June 23, 1972, was the biggest day of my life. It had been a long time since Tom and I had been altar boys waiting in the sacristy for the priest to get everything ready for mass.

"Relax," he said. "Jan's a great girl, and you guys make a great couple. What else could you ask for?"

He was right, and his words settled me down. I didn't "fall" in love with Janine. I liked her more and more, and then eased into loving her over the preceding two years. The first year of medical school was behind us, and in a few minutes, we would be married. Jim would lose a roommate but gain a brother-in-law.

"Tom, do I look alright, really?"

I had contact lenses now, and I had done my best to smash my hair into a part.

"Let me put it this way; you look about as good as you can," he answered.

"Thanks, I think."

We both laughed. We needed each other again. This was tough for both of us for different reasons. He was a proud man, and though he was pretty much resigned to his chair, it still hurt him to be in it. I knew it was hard for him out in front of the church using a transfer board to slide out of the car and into the wheelchair while wearing a tuxedo. It would be tough for him to be in front of two hundred friends and relatives in a few minutes, but he knew how important it was for Janine and me to have him with us for this moment.

"Rich," he said with his Walter Reed/Cleveland Rehab serious face on, which always told me whatever he was going to say next would be important. "I want to thank you for asking me to be your best man."

In seconds, the whole time I had known him flashed through my head, from soaping windows on Halloween to this moment. I had either to say something sarcastic or breakdown on the spot. The priest had stepped out for a second.

"Who the hell else would I ask, you Goddamn horse's ass?" I said to him, just as the priest reappeared in the doorway. It was okay. We were ready.

I wheeled Tom out to his spot next to me, and we, Jim, and my brother, Walt, watched as Janine came down the aisle on her father's arm. When I looked at her face, any doubts I had disappeared. We had found each other at the perfect time, and we were very good for each other. When we were together, we were happy. When we weren't, we got by, but it wasn't the same.

We said our vows, exchanged rings, and were pronounced man and wife. We kissed and turned to face our families and friends. It was the happiest moment of my life.

We had planned it for a year, and it came off perfectly. Tom toasted us, and caught the garter by parking a wheel on it when it hit the floor. Everybody ate, drank, danced, and laughed. It was a celebration of love and being alive.

CHAPTER 8

There were certain things about me that Janine became aware of early on and adjusted to. Some were voluntary behaviors, like how I would not move things curiously or conspicuously out of place on the sidewalk or in public places because of my experiences with booby traps and their triggering devices. And how I slept with my right leg out of my poncho liner and now bedcovers so I wouldn't get tangled up if somebody tried to sneak up and slit my throat. Others were involuntary and could not be suppressed, like nightmares that scared her too, and my reaction to being startled, which was startling to others. Also, we went camping with a pup tent a few times, but after I nearly tore it apart trying to get out when I heard a noise in the darkness, we didn't do that anymore.

Then there were the annual searches for Word's family to tell them what their son had done for me, and give them any other information they might want about what happened that day, like Tom's friend had done. I felt I owed that to Bill. There was one other situation I needed closure on. After leaving Vietnam and taking a thirty day leave, I had to return to Schoffield Barracks and serve my last three months before discharge. I shared a cubicle in a squad bay with Jeff Moyer, another 9th Infantry Division soldier who was part of the first pullout. We became friends and a source of support for each other in the difficult environment of a peace time army unit after being in war. He had two-and-half years left to serve and chose to go back to Vietnam and fight again rather than shine brass and polish shoes every day. We exchanged a few letters after that, and then one night on the 6:30 news, they showed his outfit cut off and outnumbered by a North Vietnamese Army unit. There were no more letters. I needed to know whether he was dead or alive, but I had no success on numerous attempts to find him or his family.

Other than that, I liked that medicine has no age, gender, or geographic borders. We may look different, speak different languages, and have different customs and cultures, but we all have the same anatomy and physiology and are subject to the same diseases and conditions that threaten our well-being and cause death. Those are the enemies; all human beings face and fight them. We may grieve the loss of a loved one differently, but the pain of it is universal. In learning how to heal others, I was being healed. It was a better mission than "if he moves, Doc, kill 'im."

Time passed and life just got better and better. Vice President Spiro Agnew resigned and pleaded no contest to criminal charges confirming him as the most corrupt vice-president in history. Nixon resigned to escape impeachment for the abuses of power discovered in the process of investigating the Watergate scandal, and then Gerald Ford, who Nixon picked to replace Agnew, pardoned him. It would take me decades to accept that act as the contribution to this country's well-being that it was. That Sunday morning he announced it, I hit the median on Michigan Avenue while driving home to married housing with a bag of fresh bagels. Oh yeah, then Saigon fell and the war ended.

I graduated from medical school, passed my licensure exam, and Janine and I moved to Milwaukee for my family practice residency at St. Luke's Hospital. We got a puppy from the humane society. He was a Labradoodle, but the breed had not been "discovered" yet, so he was just a big mutt, one-hundred-ten pounds-worth by his first birthday. We couldn't believe how smart he appeared to be. During housebreaking, O'Reilly peed on the newspaper I laid out for him only one time. I guess it made it too hard for him to read, so he never did it again. He trained us that when he went to the door and stood there, he needed to go out. If we didn't respond, he would give a single, soft, indignant "woof."

There were some scary moments health-wise with Janine's dad that year, so we decided to move back to Michigan and do the last two years of residency at Sparrow Hospital in Lansing. Before we left, Janine had a nice party thrown for her at the neurology rehab place where she had logged four-thousand volunteer hours in a year. They congratulated her on a job well done and on her announcement that she was pregnant.

On February 19, 1977, Kathleen Grace was born healthy and beautiful. She was named for Janine and Jim's deceased sister and their father's mother. I finished my residency on June 30, 1978, passed my exam for board certification in family practice, and opened my solo family practice office with obstetrics on July 10, 1978. On August 30, 1978, we welcomed our second healthy and beautiful daughter, Meegan Marie, into the world.

My practice was thriving, Janine was a full-time mom and we had our own home. Life was everything any of us ever hoped it would be.

I accepted an invitation to become a member of the Legislative Committee of the Ingham County Medical Society because I thought it might help me overcome my aversion to politics. Once a month during the legislative session, we would breakfast with the local lawmakers and offer the doctors' side on important medical-related issues. I was meeting good people who were dedicated to representing their constituents well. That helped me.

On October 30, 1980, I attended a conference on the future of health care delivery in this country. It was obvious that the federal government would continue to take greater control of healthcare, and politics would play a central role in decision making. Those decisions would directly impact my career and my ability to provide for my family.

The conference was presented by The Michigan State Medical Society, and the speakers included an official of the American Hospital Association, the head of the American Medical Association, and a foremost supply-side economics theorist. There were several hundred doctors from across the state in attendance. Much to my surprise, I was enjoying the conference more than I thought I would. At the end of the program, the keynote speaker was introduced.

"Ladies and gentlemen, we are pleased to have with us today as a guest of the Michigan State Medical Society, United States Senator Carl Levin, Democrat from Michigan, who will be speaking to us about issues in medicine at the national level. Senator Levin is a member of the Senate Armed Services Committee, and..."

Those were the last words I heard. It wasn't a simple flashback; I was on ground in Rach Kien, Vietnam unable to breath and holding my guts in while hearing everybody screaming for me to come help them. I broke out in a sweat and started to feel lightheaded and my breathing got shallow. I looked around the room and tried to re-orient. I could see and hear the Senator speaking, but it was like I wasn't really there. I am not certain how long it took for me to refocus and think rationally. As a member of the Armed Services Committee, Levin might be able to help me find Word's family and learn the fate of Moyer. It never entered my mind that these events happened over ten years earlier. I started writing a note to Senator Levin on the back of the conference program asking for his help. There wasn't much space to write in and there wasn't much time. I almost gave it up, but then I started drifting back to that place, and it made me write faster.

I was crying and shaking by the time I had the opportunity to personally hand the note to the Senator after the conference. He took one look at me, put his hand on my shoulder, and we walked over to some chairs. He read it and then tried to help me get it together. He told me that he understood and would try to help. I was impressed by his compassion and sincerity. I was impressed by something else: the feelings that had just surfaced and their intensity. I was simultaneously embarrassed, humiliated, and confused.

A couple of weeks later, my next door neighbor, Peter, a professor of American History at MSU, asked me if I would be willing to speak to one of his classes about the Vietnam War as part of the wrap up of several sessions they had spent on it. He thought the material would come alive and be more meaningful that way. After what happened at the leadership conference, I decided it might be best to re-open a personal dialogue on the war and smooth any rough spots that apparently remained. I said yes.

He spoke for thirty minutes and wrapped up with some parallels between Vietnam and America's newest advisory mission in Central America. When he introduced me, I came to the front of the room.

I started off okay. I tried to bring home the fact that I had sat in this building just as they were doing. I told them that I had listened to the President of the United States as the war in Southeast Asia became our war, then my war, then nobody's war. I told them about Tom and Word and the kids in the school bus. I could hear my voice involuntarily cracking and became aware that my eyes were wet. I had to stop for a moment because I knew I was starting to lose it. Then I tried to make one last point.

"You had better form an opinion about this Contra versus Sandinista thing in Nicaragua. It might not look like much to you now, and you may think you're too busy to pay attention to it, but when it drags your ass out of this room and you're trying to tell the good guys from the bad guys while your friends are being blown apart, it will be too late."

The room was quiet except for the soft sobbing of a girl who had lost a brother in Vietnam. Some asked questions, which I did my best to answer. Then the class was over, Peter thanked me, and the students applauded. I could see why Peter was a popular prof. I found myself out in the crowded hallway, flowing along in a river of students hurrying to wherever, consumed with the task of making it in 1981, just as we had been in 1966.

"On three, okay?" I said to Kathleen and Meegan. "O'Reilly, sit. Stay." He was as excited as the girls, but he obeyed.

I had raked the fallen leaves into a massive pile. The girls and the dog couldn't wait to jump into it.

"Okay, one, two, THREE!"

The two of them took off as fast as they could. O'Reilly whined and then barked.

"GO!" I said to him.

All three dove into the leaves, and I followed them. In a few minutes, the pile was leveled.

"I'll rake them up into a pile again. Kathleen, go get Mom for the next one, and you need to give Meegan a head start next time."

"Okay," she answered.

I restacked, and everybody was ready. I didn't even try to make O'Reilly wait.

"Okay, one…"

Before I said "two," Janine grabbed up Meegan and ran for the pile, and the dog followed.

"No fair, you cheated!" Kathleen complained as she and I ran after them.

We rolled around, hugging each other and throwing leaves in the air while O'Reilly climbed all over us.

"Again, again!" he girls squealed.

"Okay," I said as I grabbed the rake, and Janine went back in the house to check on what she was cooking.

A few minutes later, she came to the door.

"Telephone, Rich. It's Senator Levin."

I dropped the rake and ran in.

"Rich, I'm having difficulty getting information on Moyer. Is there anything more you can tell me about him?"

All we had was his name, the outfit we were in at Schoffield, that he used to loan me a pair of gym shorts with Rockport Athletics written on them, and that he was from Illinois.

"Could it have been Rockford?" the senator asked.

"No, I'm positive it was Rockport. I called the high school and the swim coach there the first few years after I got out, but no one knew him."

"Okay. Also, I have found some information on a next of kin for Word, but this one was not from West Virginia. Could you be wrong on that?"

"Yeah, I could. Things were pretty hectic back then."

"Okay. I just wanted to let you know that I was working on this. I'll continue and keep you posted."

"Thank you, Sir. Your help means a lot to me."

"Goodbye, Rich."

Janine went outside alone.

"Where's Dad? We want to do it again," the girls said. "Dad's tired and needs to take a rest. Anyway, it's time to eat."

"Richard, I have a pair of tickets to a one-hundred-dollar-a-plate Republican fundraiser on an estate in Williamston. They're yours if you want them."

It was late fall, 1981. Kevin Kelly and I were between pickup games in MacDonald Middle school gym where aging neighborhood basketball freaks played on Tuesday nights. He worked for the Michigan State Medical Society as their legislative liaison. I admired him as human being and was proud to call him my friend.

"I think I'd rather walk through hell with gasoline drawers on, Kevin, but thanks any way."

"It's a steak dinner, and the guest of honor is going to be Gerald R. Ford."

I told him about my obscene fantasy regarding what Ford did for Nixon to get appointed vice president. He laughed.

"Well, now's your chance to ask him about that."

I don't think the valet parked many other 1980 Ford Fiestas that night. There was no way to confirm that; the parking area for the five-hundred people in attendance was in a remote area of the estate.

"Are you sure you're going to be okay?" Janine asked as we walked toward the main house.

"I thought so until I saw that," I said as I nodded my head toward

Ford's mode of conveyance to the event.

"You mean that helicopter?" she asked.

"That's a Huey, the work horse of Vietnam. I've never seen one painted up so pretty. It looks like Charles Bronson in drag."

"We can leave if you want," she said.

"I'm hungry; let's stay."

We were in a huge tent. People in fashionable clothes and glittering jewelry talked and laughed in groups of varying sizes, holding drinks brought around by waiters, and being serenaded by strolling violinists while photographers' strobes flashed all over the place. After a while, we all took seats at large round tables. As the band played, a bevy of state Republican officials paraded across the stage followed by the guest of honor. A local cleric delivered an invocation, and the five-hundred people were served filet mignon, hot.

After that, it was time for the guest of honor to update us on current events, like golfing with Bob Hope, the trouble with the Carter Administration, and the great things in store for the Republican Party, the state, and the nation, thanks to generous folks like us. Then he and Betty left as the crowd stood and clapped. I was the last to stand and I didn't clap. I never got past the fact that an ex-commander-in-chief was using a Huey to fly to a high-priced Republican fundraiser. The first time I saw a Huey land, I was in line to give blood to its passengers. The only time I was in one was after the cluster fuck. When I was with the 9th Aviation Battalion, ones that got shot down were brought there by flying cranes for repair or salvage.

In addition, this man pardoned Nixon for crimes against the American people that I thought he should have been executed for. I made a mistake coming to this; I made a bigger one signing the guest register.

Back in the car, Janine broke the silence.

"Do you want to talk about it, Rich?"

"No."

Senator Levin's next call came shortly after.

"Rich, how are you doing?" he asked.

"I'm hangin' in, Sir, how are you?"

"I'm doing well, and I have some news for you. First off, Jeff Moyer's records were destroyed in the fire at the National Archives in St Louis in 1973. There is no way to find out anything further about him."

"Okay."

"Now, hear me out on this before you say anything. I have found a next of kin of Bill Word."

The familiar chill went through my entire body.

"Here's how it works regarding possible contact between you and them, and the rules on this are very strict. You send a letter to me with what you would like to say to them, I forward it, they respond to me as to whether or not they want to communicate further with you, and then I contact you. Are you clear on this?"

"Yes, Sir, I've got it. I'll send a letter to you right away. Thank you. I can't believe it."

"Well, don't get your hopes up too high, but go ahead and put down what you need to say and I'll forward it as soon as I receive it."

"I will, and Senator, no matter how it goes, I will never forget what you have done for me. Thank you again."

"You're welcome, Rich, I'm happy I could be of assistance. Goodbye."

"Goodbye."

A few weeks later, he called back.

"Rich, Word's next of kin do not wish to make a contact with you. That's all I can tell you, and this is where it ends. I'm sorry, I know how you must feel, but you have to respect their rights and understand. It's been a long time, Rich, and apparently they have healed and don't want to go back to a painful time. You need to move on, too. Are you okay?"

"Part of me understands and part of me probably never will. I'll figure it out, I guess, someday."

"Hopefully, we all will," he answered. "Good luck."

"Same to you, Senator; keep doing what you do, and how you go about it. It means a lot to people. Goodbye."

"Goodbye, Rich."

I was unaware that signing the guest book at the Ford fundraiser would add my name to the Republican Senate Select Mailing list. The materials I subsequently received gave me a new level of insight into the role of money in the political process and the shameless pandering done to obtain it. The most troubling was dated July 23, 1982. It began with "Dear Friend," ended with "make check payable to," and was signed "Sincerely, Ronald Reagan." Included was a survey that assured my input in the formulation of important policy decisions. This one crossed the line separating junk mail from something uglier. It mocked citizenship, the intelligence of the electorate, and the office of President of the United States of America. It forced me to response in kind.

I sent a letter to President Reagan apologizing for not completing the National Legislative Action Survey before the August 23, 1982, deadline because I was unable to answer a single question on it. I told him how upsetting that was for me because I had spent time in a country where the citizens were not interested enough in their government, and as a result the country no longer exists.

I told him how it made me feel to get a letter from Washington DC from someone I'd never met that began with "Dear Friend," and that I had come there in 1968 to visit my best friend at Walter Reed after he had been rendered quadriplegic in Vietnam.

I concluded by asking him to put me up at his place for a few days so I could get his answers to the survey, meet with some Democrats to get theirs, and then give him mine. After that, I would give him a crack at my wallet. I reminded him: "you wrote to me first."

What did I hope to accomplish? I needed affirmation that this is indeed a government of the people, for the people, and by the people, and that what's in your heart is more valuable than what's in your wallet. I needed to be reassured that the America I, my friends, and our ancestors fought to preserve, was still alive. I didn't like being used. Presidents should not do that to citizens. That's what Nixon did.

Two months later, I got a reply from the Chairman of the Republican National committee thanking me for my letter and informing me that employment was up, inflation down, and "your comments are always welcome."

This was getting serious. It is not safe for representative government to be this out of touch with the people it's supposed to represent. I sent the non-reply back with a copy of my original letter, and asked that the issues I raised be addressed. After three months without a reply, I took a different tack. At the end of the weekly meeting of my office staff, I brought up some new business.

"I want to form an organization of the five of us."

They wanted more details; I reassured them: "this will require nothing on your part; just trust me on this."

They were confused, but they agreed.

"Now, I want the organization to think about donating $100,000 to the re-election of Ronald Reagan."

They were shocked.

"Just think about what I just said, that's all."

They did.

"Okay, thanks; meeting adjourned."

I sent the following letter the same day.

"Dear Mr. Reagan:

I am a member of an organization contemplating a $100,000

donation to your re-election campaign. Would you please furnish details on how to proceed with implementation?"

I received a two-page letter from one of two deputy counsels of the Republican National Committee with the details and a phone number if I had any further questions.

I had heard all I needed to hear from my "dear friends" in Washington, but the materials kept coming. If I got "on board," I could get "President Reagan's specially commissioned golden Medal of Merit, a beautiful and positive way to show you're working to make a better America." I thought the Purple Heart did that. For a few more bucks, I could get my name inscribed on "the President's Honor Roll and be kept forever with his permanent Presidential Papers." No, thanks; I had friends who gave their lives for this country, and you don't need to rummage around in Ronald Reagan's basement to see their names. They're engraved on a black granite wall down the street from the White House.

Something was drastically wrong here. As an American citizen, I don't need a $100,000 megaphone to be heard by an elected official at any level of government. The Constitution guarantees me that right and binds them to that responsibility. As a people, we love freedom and see democracy as the best way to assure it no matter what the personal cost. That's the America my friends and our fathers put our lives on the line to defend. I found measuring my love for my country by how many dollars I am willing to contribute to a candidate running for an elected office disgusting.

Simultaneously, the government that sent my friends and I into a bad war in Southeast Asia, was now manufacturing justifications for an eerily similar one in Central America. I concluded that the President needed to know what government looked and sounded like down here at the bottom, and if we were going to be buddies, I wanted to introduce him to some of my other friends.

I was a busy practicing physician, husband, and father. I did not have the time, energy, or expertise to write a book, but this had to be done.

The power of the government of this country to do great things was only matched by its power to ruin lives. It all depended on its orientation and right then, I saw that as wrong.

To write about war was to relive it. I walled myself in and when not totally immersed in the task, I was still not fully a part of my family. I found fault with everything and everybody around me. I ceased to be a partner. I wasn't the father I should have been. The marriage suffered.

"That's just the way things are and have always been. You can't change that, let it go," friends who meant well would say to me. "Do you actually believe it's worth what you're doing to yourself and your family?"

I knew where I needed to go to find the answer.

I made my way through the terminal and found myself outside. It was hot, about ninety degrees, and very humid. I flagged a cab and got in.

"Where to, Buddy?"

"The Vietnam Memorial."

It had been sixteen years since I had come to Washington to see Tom at Walter Reed. I couldn't bring myself to look around the area in 1968; today I could.

"Right over there," the driver motioned.

I paid him and got out. There was the shinning, white, multi-pillared Lincoln Memorial to my right and the gleaming white Washington Memorial reaching skyward to my left. Between them, like a black scar in the ground, was the Vietnam Memorial.

I sat down on a nearby bench to get a feeling for the place. It was peaceful. I could not say it was beautiful; it just seemed to fit. A helicopter was passing over. No need to look up, it was a Huey. I felt suspended somewhere between the past and present but not really part of either. I heard someone mention a directory, and I went and found it. I flipped to the "w's" and was stunned to find Word's hometown listed as Sunnyvale, California. I appreciated Carl Levin even more. The directory showed which of the seventy panels his name was inscribed on, and what line on the panel.

Next, I looked for Moyer. There were several, but no Jeff. I looked slowly and carefully again; he did not die in Vietnam. I didn't know anything more about him, but that was good enough. I found Benjamin Harrison and wrote down his numbers, and likewise Robert Freeman.

I closed the directory, took my numbers and my bags, and headed back down the walkway. As the path descended, the black granite panels rose higher, covered with more and more names, listed without rank, in the order in which they had been killed. When I reached panel twenty-three, I stopped. At the start of line thirteen, I found Word. My head stuffed up and my eyes ran. I stepped to the base of the panel and tried to touch his name but couldn't. I stood on my toes and stretched as far and as hard as I could, and then I jumped. Just like before, I could not get to him. I turned, put my back against the wall, slid to the ground, and buried my face in my hands. Someone I never looked up at put his hand on my shoulder and said, "It's okay, man, it's okay." After a few seconds, I looked up, and there was no one there. I got back on my feet, stared up at Word's name, and photographed it.

Fifty-one lines below was Benjamin Harrison. I had prayed so hard that he wouldn't die, and he tried so hard to live. I knew him for about an hour, and even though he never knew me, he will always be part of my life. I touched and photographed his name.

On the panel just to the left of Word and Harris, I found Robert Freeman. I never knew him as a soldier. We were "boys from Brougham," students, assholes, but there he was. Somehow, he had gotten into the war and was killed. Like the others, I touched his name and photographed it.

Then I stood there for a long time, alternately relieved that I did not have to talk to anyone, then feeling as though I'd go to pieces if I didn't. Behind me, people came and went, and I could hear parts of conversations.

"He was the nicest kid you ever could have wanted to meet."

"I think it's just an awesome monument, so right."

"Why did somebody shoot your friend, Daddy?"

"One lousy week, that was all he had left."

After a while, I walked back up the grade and laid down on the grass under a tree across from the wall. I stayed there until it was dark to make sure the place still felt safe and peaceful. Then I left.

Not long after the trip, Janine and I separated.

"I really think it would be more productive to change our approach for this counseling from conjoined to individual, at least for a little while."

We had been meeting with a good psychologist, Dr. Joseph McKendry, who came highly recommended by friends. I had talked with him a couple of times at nurses' stations in the hospital over the years and enjoyed those informal contacts.

"Would you both be agreeable to that?"

"I would be," Janine answered.

"That sounds like a good idea to me, too."

"Good. Then Rich, you and I will be meeting together for the immediate future."

"I thought you meant you and Janine."

"No, Rich. You have had some experiences that are your own, but they strongly influence your dealings with others. I think that is where the emphasis needs to be for now."

"I know I have some issues, but I don't think they are the primary problem in this relationship," I said.

"And that's exactly where you and I will start next time," he answered.

I thought we were on the wrong track, but I would listen and try it.

"Rich, what is your understanding of Post-Traumatic Stress

Disorder?" he asked after a couple of sessions.

"That's what Veterans who sit around drinking and smoking themselves to death while telling the same war stories to each other have," I told him.

"That may be true in some extreme cases, but obviously not in yours," he answered.

"I don't think I have that."

"Can you tell me why not?"

"I was only there a short time, and I was a medic. My job was to help. Bad things happened to me, but others had it much worse or even died. I came home, finished college and went to medical school, and now I'm a practicing doctor. I'm trying to write a book because I think the government of this country is selling out to the highest bidder and leading us into another bad war."

"Those are positive and helpful things to a certain degree, but you started college the day after your discharge from the service, you have not taken more than a week off since, and you write between 11 p.m. and 2 a.m. I do not want to get hung up in semantics or terminology, but there is something wrong with this picture."

"I totally agree."

"But the problem is not out there. It's inside you, and until you stop denying that it exists, you won't solve it, no matter how many hours you work or how many pages you write. The world already knows that war is a bad thing. You have to stop thinking about what it did to Bill, Tom, or anybody else, and focus on understanding what it did, and what you are still letting it do, to you, and how that affects your relationships with people in your life now."

I had never thought of the problem from that perspective.

"I volunteered for the draft, to go to Vietnam, and to stay after I was wounded. I asked for everything that happened to me, and I promised myself I would never let Vietnam be the excuse for anything in my life - good, bad, or indifferent."

"And in the process, you sentenced yourself to perpetuating a pattern of behavior and outcomes that has not served your best interest. It's time you rethink your position. I know you are an excellent physician, but no matter how good you are, or how much better you may become, you won't be able to accomplish what I see you trying to do."

"And what's that?"

"You can't raise the dead."

I felt the familiar whole body chill, and the hair on my arms stood up.

"Had you been there longer, you may have become somewhat desensitized to it. I liked your analogy that you were still burping stuffed cabbage when you were asked to give blood on your arrival in Vietnam. You never had the chance to adapt, and I think you are still trying to."

I thought about what he was saying before responding.

"I cannot accept the premise that something went wrong with me in Vietnam. What went wrong was our country's old script for war. Vietnam should have been the end of bad policy killing good soldiers, but I don't think it was. Two-hundred-forty-one US Marines were recently blown up in their beds in a barracks in Lebanon by two pick-up trucks loaded with explosives, and now Reagan is ready to involve us in a civil war in Nicaragua. And you think *I* have a problem because shit like that keeps me having nightmares?"

"Yes, I do."

I self-published "The President and Some of My Other Friends" in April, 1985. That June, my father walked into my office with a nine-day headache and a little sagging on the left side of his face. He died of his malignant brain tumor in November 8, 1985. The usual interpersonal issues that affect all marriages existed between Janine and me, but my inability to accept and deal effectively with the diagnosis of PTSD was also a contributing factor. The divorce ending our thirteen year marriage was final on April 18, 1986.

CHAPTER 9

I was twelve years into a solid second marriage when we moved out to the country in March, 1999. Kathleen and Meegan had just graduated from college, and Amy, my stepdaughter, was a junior in high school. Amanda, born to us in 1989, was in grammar school. My wife, Ellen, had been the manager of my solo private office until I closed it in 1992. She knew first-hand how difficult being a family doctor was. Now, I was working in a hospital-owned office, and the docs had just been given an ultimatum: you have three months to be on pace to reach national productivity benchmarks for income generation or lose your jobs. It would only get harder. Moving out here was my family's way of saying you've earned this.

As I maneuvered the huge lawn mowing machine in and out of the tall pines that lined the gravel driveway, I saw my wife coming out of the house with a drink for me. She waved, and I waved back - a bad idea because it took both hands on levers to steer. It swerved into the trees and a branch knocked my hat and my sound-deadening earmuffs into my lap. I regained control, backed up, and shut down.

"Oops," I said when she got close.

"Yeah, I've been watching. You were doing great until then. Are you okay?"

She tried not to, but as she handed me the glass of lemonade, she broke out laughing. I just looked at her. I love to look at her face, especially when she's laughing. She was usually pretty serious.

"Yeah, I'm okay; at least I'm dry this time."

Memorial Day weekend I had sunk the mower in the pond while

trying to cut weeds on a steep bank. Pop's Towing fished it out, and the boys from the farm equipment place in town fixed it. When they called to say that it was done, they asked if we wanted them to install a life preserver on it.

"This being a farmer is harder than it looks," she said.

"I guess. I've yet to shake somebody's hand out here with all five fingers on it."

While I sipped the lemonade, we savored the moment: the bright sun in a cloudless blue sky, the sweet smell of the fresh cut grass, and the songs of a dozen species of birds. Down the hill, the pond sparkled like a private sea of diamonds.

As a kid, I used to draw pictures of what my ultimate place to live might look like. It would be in the country on about fifty acres of rolling land with the house set back off the road on a hill. There would be a stream somewhere on it, some woods, a pond, and all kinds of wildlife around. I would put feed out near the house so deer and raccoons would come up close when they learned it was safe. Maybe over time, some would even learn to come when called. This was that place.

Out of the woods came Rudy, our three-year-old yellow lab. When he spotted his favorite human, he broke into a dead run. Ellen sat down on the grass and braced herself. He did a few high-speed figure eights around her, and then rolled on his back at her feet. He put his head in her lap, and she wrapped her arms around his thick neck and hugged him.

"How's my handsomest boy?" she said to him.

Rudy wagged his tail and licked her face.

"Isn't this something?" she asked as she looked around.

"Beautiful," I answered without taking my eyes off her.

It was week two of my vacation. We had stayed home. There was no reason to go anyplace else. I finished my final pass mowing around the pond. Amanda was in the rowboat, and Rudy sat on the front seat trying to keep his balance. I nodded her way and smiled. She waved and nearly lost an oar – must be genetic.

As I neared the house, I saw Ellen coming down the hill with the cordless phone in her hand and a look of concern on her face. I was on vacation; I had good coverage. Patients and friends to whom I had given my unlisted home number possessed it with the understanding that rarely I might be reachable but unavailable. This was one of those rare moments. I shut down when I reached her.

"It's Lynn from the office. She said she's sorry, but she needs to talk to you right away. She sounds upset."

I was sure this could be handled in a few seconds.

"Hi, Lynn, what's up?"

Lynn had been replaced on the other end of the line.

"This is agent Vanderlaan of the Federal Bureau of Investigation. We are in your office seizing charts; you need to come in here."

I called my superiors and they confirmed this was not a joke. We had no idea what was going on. Ellen and I got Amanda off the pond and woke Amy, and then we headed into the office.

The waiting room should have been packed with patients the morning of June 29, 1999, but it was empty. Through the sliding glass window, I could see six unusually large men in suits: one in the hallway outside the office area with my visibly shaken office staff; the other five were in the chart racks removing records.

I turned to my wife.

"Somebody messed up, all right. You better wait out here, Ellen. I don't think this will take long."

I walked through the waiting room and joined the crowd behind the glass.

"Which one of you guys is Vanderlaan?" I asked.

The largest of the strangers turned to face me.

"I am."

Whoa, I thought. I may have seen an offensive lineman or professional wrestler bigger than this guy in the past, but right now, I couldn't picture one.

"I'm Doctor Czop; would you mind telling me what the hell is going on here?"

"Let's go to a room where we can talk privately."

We walked down the hall and turned into the first exam room. He closed the door behind us.

"Doctor, you've been charged in federal court with a felony punishable by up to four years in prison. The charges stem from an investigation into fraudulently issuing time off to General Motors employees in exchange for money. Since bills and disability forms go through the mail, this constitutes mail fraud, which is a federal offense. This document delineates the nature of the investigation and the formal charges."

This was about *me*? This was crazy. I'd never done anything like that. He handed over the papers. I sat on the wheeled stool at the end of the exam table and began reading.

There was a list of seventeen of my patients, all of whom were auto workers in the General Motors plants in Lansing. I was very familiar with all but a couple because either their medical problems were serious, or their motivation to work was questionable on occasion. For some of them, it was both, and I expended a great deal of time and effort on their care, but I had never sold time off to anybody. The thought had never entered my mind, let alone "devised a plan to." Someone had made a big mistake - that's all this was. In a moment, I would explain that to Vanderlaan-the-Giant then drive back home and finish mowing the lawn. I was on vacation.

When I came to the last two pages, I froze. There in black and white were the transcribed notes for two office calls made by a man I had taken on as a new patient a couple of years earlier. The first visit started off a little shaky, but ended okay. At the second visit, if I had found the scalpel I looked for in the drawer, I might have used it to kill him. I had hoped one of the worst moments of my life would stay my secret and I would never see him again. He was the undercover investigator for the case.

Ellen had suggested I call a buddy of mine who happens to be a great attorney specializing in malpractice defense. I didn't think it was necessary at the time, but now I was glad I listened to her. Vanderlaan was about to read me my rights when there was a knock on the door.

"Come in." I didn't think to ask if it was okay for me to say that.

"Hi, Doc."

"Hi, Hack."

"I'm Randy Hackney, Dr. Czop's attorney, and you are?"

"I'm agent Vanderlaan with the FBI."

"Can you tell me what's going on here?"

"The doctor has been charged in Federal Court with-"

Randy had heard enough.

"May I see the formal complaint?"

I handed the papers to him, and the room fell silent again, except for Randy occasionally turning a page as he read.

"I'd like to talk privately with my client for a few minutes if you don't mind."

"That's okay," Vanderlaan answered.

Randy and I met Ellen in the hallway, and the three of us went into my office and closed the door.

"I've got to tell you this is serious stuff," he began.

Any remaining doubt of that after seeing six FBI agents going through my patient charts was eliminated by the expression on Randy's usually smiling face. He proceeded to tell Ellen what we had just learned. As she listened intently, her expression never changed. He turned back to me, now seated at my desk.

"What do you know about this? Do you remember this guy they planted in here?"

"Yeah, I do."

"Give me the story."

"I saw him twice. At his first visit, he wanted medical coverage for missing work. He said he got stressed out and took a few days off and played golf. I reviewed his history and decided the guy could use a break. I took him on as a new patient and covered his absence. I told him that in the future, he needed to come in before being so stressed out that he felt he needed to miss work. There was a copy of that note in what they just showed me."

"What did you put down for his diagnosis?" Ellen asked.

"Situational stress," I answered.

"Then what happened?" Randy asked.

"Nothing. He goes a year-and-a-half with no contact whatsoever with the office: no visits, no requests for coverage, not even a phone call.

"At the second visit, he was a totally different person. He told me that he lied to the receptionist on the phone to get on the schedule, he was going to go play golf in North or South Carolina with his buddies, and that I was going to cover him for it. Then he said 'it felt real good last time, Doc' and got this shit-eating grin on his face. I wanted to throw him out, but I quickly got the feeling he was on the edge of something and maybe about to go over it. I didn't want to push and have him take somebody else with him.

"So what did you do?" Ellen asked.

I couldn't call the police just because I felt threatened, and he wasn't out there far enough to consider commitment options, so I decided to kiss his ass, get him the hell out of here, and get him out of his workplace. We could work on his head later. I was *buying* time, not selling it."

"That doesn't sound unreasonable," Randy said.

"It's not, but it gets a little shitty from there."

"You didn't give him a dozen golf balls did you?" Randy asked.

"Worse."

"Uh-oh." he added.

"I couldn't use 'going to play golf' as his diagnosis, so I wrote that he had an acute flare of a chronic back problem.

"Damn. Why did you lie? Why didn't you just say situational stress again?" Ellen asked.

"The hospital isn't getting reimbursed for that diagnosis anymore, and they've warned us not to use it.

The room was silent.

"I thought this guy might go out to his car, get a shotgun out of the trunk, and come back in blasting if I didn't do something to prevent it. What's the worst thing happens with my plan? GM loses a week of this guy's pay? It cost Ford Motor Company a hell of a lot more to clean up the Wixom Plant after that nut shot the place up. What if I was right about this guy and instead of going after me, he goes home and bashes in his ex-wife's head with his three-wood, or he goes to the bar, gets tanked, then drives into some innocent person's car, maybe with one of our kids in it. I believed the potential was there."

I paused for a moment and looked at their sad, even disappointed, expressions before continuing.

"Believe it or not, under the circumstances, I actually thought I did a *good* job. Nobody got hurt, and I thought someone could. I'd have *driven* this guy *and* his friends to Myrtle Beach myself to get him the hell out of this office."

I didn't tell either of them that I had tried to arm myself with a scalpel. The room was quiet again. Then Randy spoke.

"Do you recognize any of the other names on the list?"

"All but a couple; they were all sick or injured, and it's well documented."

"Wow," Randy shook his head. I was just up the road when I got the page to come over here. I was expecting a stripper or something. Then, when I drove in and saw a car with government plates, then another, and another, I just said, 'oh shit.' Rich, I've got to tell you this is serious stuff."

"No, this is pure, unadulterated bullshit." I answered. "If they didn't like something that I was doing, couldn't they just have said, hey, we have a problem with you, or with this, or that? Pulling something like this attacks my whole family. It's not just wrong; it's sick."

Ellen and Randy were silent. I caught a breath, and then started right back in.

"Yes, I lied, but I lied to save my and the staff's asses. I thought we were in danger, and I didn't see any other reasonable options. I was guilty of nothing more than defusing a scary situation. I knew that sleazy son of a bitch was trouble, and I was dead right about that. It just never crossed my mind that this could just be somebody's big fucking joke."

"Hang in there, Czopper; I'll help you get through this, but it's a criminal matter, and that's out of my area of expertise. The hospital owns this practice and pays you a salary, right; you're an employee, not an independent contractor?"

"Right."

"This guy never gave you money?"

"Hell no; I never see money. My pay is even directly deposited by the hospital into my checking account. He paid the receptionist for his two visits and I have no input on the fee."

"I don't see how they could charge you with selling time off."

"Join the club," I answered.

Randy was silent for a moment.

"You're probably entitled to legal representation by the hospital's attorneys, but I'd strongly advise you to get your own lawyer in this situation. Their team will be acting in the best interest of the hospital. If that means cutting you lose, you're gone."

"Okay."

"Kent Haverman is the best I know to handle something like this. I'll give him a call. Otherwise, I don't think you need to be here any longer."

After Randy checked with Vanderlaan, the three of us left the building. We stopped and talked out front.

"I'll give you a buzz later tonight and see how you're doing. I'm sorry this happened to you, but we'll get through it. Ellen, don't let him do anything stupid, and make him keep his mouth shut, to the extent that's possible."

"Have you got anything easier?"

After the drive back home was underway, it was Ellen who broke the silence.

"I'm sorry, Rich."

"Why should you be sorry? You didn't do anything wrong; I did.

Well, actually, I didn't, but that doesn't matter. I don't know; this goddamn job is impossible."

"Listen, I know you. They don't. This is wrong, but whatever happens, we have each other, and nothing can change that."

Before I could savor her words, my beeper went off. I didn't recognize the number. I handed it to her, she dialed, then handed me the phone.

"Kent Haverman."

It took a second to figure out who that was.

"Oh! Yeah. Richard Czop. Hi."

"Hello, Doctor. Randy Hackney just gave me a call. We need to get together."

"When can you do it?" I asked.

"Well, where are you now?"

"We're in the car on our way back to Charlotte."

"Turn around."

"Hi, I'm Kent Haverman."

"Richard Czop, and this is my wife, Ellen."

"It's nice to meet you both, despite the circumstances. Doctor, you have an excellent reputation, and Randy Hackney is probably your biggest fan. That says something about you."

I needed to hear that. That was life as I remembered it, prior to the last couple of hours.

"Thanks. Coming from a person like Randy, that means a lot. I feel the same way about him. So does Ellen."

"I can't tell you how relieved I was to see Randy walk into that office," Ellen added.

"He makes everybody feel that way, except the plaintiff's attorney," Kent added.

I liked him already. He was at ease, and he tried to help us feel that way, but his eyes were studying us carefully. Despite my references, he would form his own opinion of me. In his world, I was a criminal. His job was to prove that I wasn't; first, to himself.

"Randy faxed me a copy of the complaint against you. Did you see this?"

"Yeah, the FBI agent showed it to me."

"I'm having a little trouble understanding this. You're accused of selling off-work slips, but it's my understanding that you're on a salary and employed by the hospital. Is that correct?"

"Yes."

"How would you profit from something like this?"

I felt safe; I unloaded.

"Look, this stuff is the biggest pain in the ass that I deal with. I take care of people, sick people. I don't care *if* they work, *where* they work, or *what* they do. If they are a danger to themselves or others in the work place, I remove them from it until I find out what's wrong with them and fix it. If there is some flaw in that, why didn't somebody just tell me? If they've got a better idea, I'll do it. If not, get the hell out of the way and let me take care of the poor slob, okay?"

"Doctor, I'm on *your* side."

"I'm sorry, Kent, but I just can't understand all this."

"Well, that's my job, and I'll try to make it clear to you as soon as it's clear to me. Basically, though, these people are out to get you. It's unlikely that you could go to jail for this, but they could fine you, get your license, take away your ability to bill federal programs like Medicare and Medicaid, or any combination of the above. What did you do to get them this bent out of shape with you?"

I paused.

"Which time?" I finally answered.

"Uh, oh," Kent replied.

"You mean like when I sat across the desk from the medical director and associate medical director of Blue Cross/Blue Shield's largest HMO in the area and told them that 'you two *are* the problem?' Or the time I had to go over the head of the State Director of the Blue Care Network to get them to pay for an MRI? Or maybe-"

"How many of these do you have?" Kent asked.

"Twenty-one years' worth," Ellen answered.

She and Kent had the same expression on their faces, a look that showed kind of an acceptance or resignation with a hint of sadness.

"And what can you tell me about the encounter with the investigator they planted in your office? Do you recall any of that?"

I proceeded to tell Kent everything that I had told Randy about it.

"I'm impressed that you can recall so clearly two visits out of, what, a few thousand, over a year and half span?"

"I had a bad feeling about the guy. I was a medic in the 9th Infantry division in Vietnam. How people looked and moved and how they made us feel were sometimes all we had to go on to tell us what we had to do. I learned to trust my gut. That and luck are why I'm still here."

"He was probably wearing a wire. Do you understand what I mean by that?"

"Yeah, the second encounter was recorded on tape. I saw the transcript today. The paperwork said the equipment failed on the first visit."

"Okay, I'll get hold of it."

"It's going to sound bad to anybody that doesn't understand what I was doing and why."

"You had your reasons, and they sound legitimate. Let me outline for you the basic direction that things will be moving."

We listened as he told us about how the wheels of justice would grind, how evidence against me had been and may still be being obtained, and what to expect from my employer. He wrapped up with advice to not give any kind of statement to the news media.

"Unbelievable," I responded.

"I'd be honored to represent you if you want me to."

"We'd be honored to have you do that," I answered as Ellen

nodded in agreement.

"Do you have any questions?" he asked.

"What about the possibility of counter-suing?" I asked.

"I was wondering when you were going to ask that. I've seen two people attempt it and both failed. You would have to go after General Motors and the Blues, and they have large, well-funded legal departments just waiting to drain every resource you have. Pull your ass out of the fire first."

The man could speak my language; I was reassured. Ellen had been listening intently and taking notes. She confirmed their accuracy with Kent. Then she asked the question I couldn't.

"What are your fees for a case like this?"

Money was never much of motivator or something I spent a lot of time thinking about. There had always been enough to cover everybody, although never much else.

"My retainer is $25,000. That may be adequate, but if things go as badly as they can in a situation like this and there's a trial, it could cost as much as $100,000. My hourly fee is $225."

"Don't worry, Rich. We'll get through this," my wife said as the ride home began.

It was hard for me to talk. Two hours earlier, I had been at the pinnacle of my personal and professional life.

"I can't believe this is happening. Where are we going to get that kind of money? We sunk everything into the new place."

We began generating scenarios for where we would move and what each of us would need to do for work. It wasn't panic, it was planning. In the fourteen years we worked together, we faced daily stresses, weekly crises, and monthly disasters. For every one, there was not just a solution, but a written policy and/or procedure to make it unlikely to recur, and easier to handle if it did. At the same time, we created a blended a family against long odds.

"Jeez, where have you guys been? We're starving. We thought you were just going be gone a little while."

"I know, Amy, we did, too. We're sorry." Ellen answered the upset sixteen-year-old.

We sat at the table and broke the news. Amy responded immediately.

"Yeah, right, and just where do they think that money is? Would it be in his Gucci wardrobe, or maybe his eight year old used car? What a bunch of crap. That really makes me mad!"

Ellen continued.

"The FBI has probably tapped our phone and been listening to our conversations and seeing our online computer work."

"Are you serious?" Amy gasped, her eyes widening. "The FBI is involved? I can't believe this. You guys hardly even use the phone. With Rich, it's either the hospital about a patient, or buddies calling to set up a tee time. Mom, you talk to your medical assistant people or your sisters. Whoever is doing the bugging probably died of boredom. I can just hear them talking this stuff over. Hey, I got a big drug score going down this week in Columbia. Well, I've got terrorists going to blow up a monument. What about you? Gee, I don't know if Amy's going to have a date or not this Saturday night, and Rich shot a ninety-two again. Really, I mean just chill, FBI. Go catch a serial killer or some terrorists or something. What's up with them anyway?"

Then it was Amanda's turn.

"Dad, can't we call the police about this?"

Everybody laughed, except Amanda. She was dead serious, and we had hurt her feelings.

"*What?*" she shouted. "Why are you laughing at me?"

"Amanda, we're not laughing at you," I said. "You don't know it, but what you said is kind of funny. The FBI *is* the police. It's like we have the police for Charlotte and Lansing? Well, the FBI is the police for the entire country."

"Oh."

"We have to tell you a few more things, and then we'll be done," Ellen went on. "This is probably going to be in the newspaper and maybe even on the TV news. If anybody asks you about it, just say that you don't know anything more than what they saw or heard and that you can't talk about it."

"Oh, that's just great." Amy shook her head then continued. "They completely screw up your life, tell the world, then you're not supposed to talk about it. Sure sounds healthy to me. Anything else you want to share with us today about life in America?" Amy added.

"Yes, there is," I answered. "This is going to be an expensive thing, and right now we don't have the kind of money it's going to cost."

"I have some money in the bank. You can have it, Dad."

"Thanks, Amanda, but you don't need to do that."

"Okay, but if you change your mind, you can have it, all of it. And those pop cans you were going to let me give to 4-H? You can have them too."

It was becoming more and more obvious that the most innocent was going to be the most affected by these events, whatever the outcome.

Ellen wrapped things up. "This is happening to all of us, and it's not going to be easy for anybody. Let's just keep talking to each other and try to help each other out, and we'll get through it."

After thinking for nearly an hour about what I would say over our possibly bugged phone, I made a call.

"Meegs, how's it going?"

"Hey, Dad, I was just going to call you. Things are going great. Finals are over, I did well, and two of my pieces were selected for this big art exhibition."

"Nice going. Congratulations. We're very proud of you."

"Thanks. And how are you guys?"

I hated to tell her, but I didn't want to put it off and have somebody hand her a newspaper.

"Dad, I'm so sorry. Is there anything I can do? Would you like me to drive up? I don't have much in the way of money, but I have a little that you can have."

"I just wanted you to know about it, and I want you to know that I didn't do what they're accusing me of."

"You didn't need to say that, I know you."

I felt my eyes moistening.

"Thanks."

"Does Kathleen know?" Meegan asked.

"No. She's going to call tomorrow; I figured I'd tell her then." I answered.

"Yeah, she'll feel terrible, but best she hears it from you before she leaves the country for two years. I love you, Dad. Hang in there, and let me know anything that happens, okay?"

"Yeah; I love you too."

The next morning, I slid the pole barn's huge side door open, climbed aboard the mower, and started it up. I eased forward on the two levers, careful to keep both hands even. Our tracks in Vietnam were steered in the same way; I remembered that fact every time I mowed, and somewhere with my army papers was my 9th Infantry Division license to drive one. Today, I remembered when I got it and what the company clerk said when I asked why I needed it.

"So you can drive the track back to base camp if everybody else gets killed," he answered without looking up from his paperwork.

"Right, we wouldn't want to make a bad day worse by me driving the track back without a license," I answered.

I drove into the bright sunlight, lowered the deck, and engaged the blades. Rudy split for parts unknown as I headed for where I had left off when the FBI called. Today, it was a different world. The nation I had once fought for had declared war on me. I couldn't help but think about infamous encounters between the FBI and dangerous citizens at places like

Ruby Ridge and Waco. I tried as objectively as I could to understand the government's actions. They made forty-four unfounded accusations against me based on the investigator's second visit. He presented as a liar and a cheat without regard for the consequences of his actions. He appeared physically ready and able to do whatever he needed to in order to get what he wanted. I felt threatened, and I took action in the face of limited available options. There were no casualties.

There wasn't a blade of grass over two- and-a-half inches tall in sight when I put the mower away and met Ellen on the deck.

"How's it going?" we simultaneously asked each other.

We laughed, and it felt good, but then the phone rang. Before, we used to just answer it, but now, with the possibility of it being bugged, no one wanted to. We weren't sure what to say. Finally, I picked it up.

"Hello?"

"Hi, Dad!" Kathleen never sounded happier.

I felt a surge of relief and joy.

"It's so good to hear your voice. How's it going?"

"Wow, thanks Dad. The group of about fifty of us spent the night in Philadelphia. The Peace Corps gave us each ninety bucks and told us to party. We had a riot. Then this morning, we were bussed up here to Kennedy Airport, but there's fog, so we're delayed a couple hours. We're having a great time."

Her degree from University of Michigan was in French, and she spoke it fluently. She would be spending the next two years teaching English to French-speaking people in Guinea, Africa. She sounded so excited and happy. I knew that what I had to tell her would change that, but there was no way around it. When I was done, she was upset.

"Do you want me to come home, Dad? I can do this later."

"No way, this is stuff on paper. We're all basically the same as when you last saw us. It's not like somebody's sick or something. You go on as planned, and I'll keep you posted. You just take care of yourself;

you're on the right track."

"But I feel so bad for you."

"Hey, I can take care of myself. I'm more worried about you than I am about this. I just wanted you to hear it first-hand. I don't need you to do anything about it."

"I can always come back if you change your mind."

"Thanks, but no. Just keep yourself safe, please."

"Okay, Dad. I love you."

"I love you, too, Kack. Don't tease the lions."

"I promise."

Friends and family rallied around us. Their love and support helped us work through the initial shock of what had taken place and helped us prepare for what would follow.

CHAPTER 10

"Good luck, Rich."

"Thanks. If I'm not back in an hour, I still have a job."

Over the weekend, the story was in the state's major newspapers and on the TV news. I was part of a statewide sting operation targeting doctors who actually were selling off-work coverage to General Motors employees. Conspicuously absent was any contact from my employer. I did my clinical clerkships in medical school at that hospital, and I completed its three-year family practice residency. For twenty-one years, I had been an active member of the medical staff. Nevertheless, I hadn't heard a word.

After the thirty minute ride, I was back at the scene of the "crime." The first thing I did was look at the sign. My name was still on it. That was step one.

I got out of the car and just stood there. My confidence was shaken. I wasn't sure if I could still do my job; I wasn't sure if I still wanted to. As I walked in the front door, I wondered about my co-workers. The raid traumatized them, and they, too, had decisions to make. Was associating with me a threat to their livelihood? Would they support me or distance themselves? The answers came quickly.

"Hi, Louise."

Our receptionist jumped out of her seat behind the glass, literally ran, and wrapped her arms around me.

"It's *so* good to see you. We missed you. It's not fun working here without you. Are you okay? Your patients have been driving us nuts. Where's Doc? Is he all right? When will he be back?"

One after the other, the entire staff came and gave me a hug and the same message: "you're going to be okay. Things will work out."

I was overwhelmed, but with my having been gone and my associate starting her vacation that day, there wasn't much time for talking. There was work to do. I took the chart off the door of room one and walked in.

"Selling time off? You? Remember after my breast cancer surgery and blood clot, I asked you for another week off, and you said, now let me see if I can get this right, *'hell no*'?"

"I did? I'm sorry, Karen."

"Don't be. You said that it was as important for my head for me to get back on the job as it was for my body to have had the cancer removed. And guess what? You were right."

I really needed to hear that kind of stuff. I had always considered myself a good doctor. I worked hard at it. Hearing it from a patient who knew first-hand was the ultimate affirmation.

Others found it laughable. Steve owned a large auto/truck dealership in the area.

"Doc?" He paused and just looked at me in disbelief, impeccable in his monogrammed white shirt and silk tie. "Just tell me one thing. Do these people know that you drove a Yugo for eight years?"

I cracked up.

"I loved that thing. It actually came with its own toolbox. First time in history they recalled the country instead of the car."

"This is crazy, but I think I know where you went wrong." Steve continued.

"Where?"

"You shouldn't have gone for the GVL, the top of the line Yugo with that sunroof and the wood grain paper on the dash."

We were both laughing.

"Yeah? You think that's what it was, huh? You know what? I had to use an umbrella inside that thing when it rained."

Steve cracked up.

"You had to go and get flashy. What'd you ever do with that thing, anyway?"

"I sold it in a yard sale for three hundred fifty bucks."

"Well, hey, seriously, if you need somebody to say some good stuff on your behalf, my family and I would love to have the opportunity. Just tell us when and where, and we'll be there. Okay?"

"Yeah, and thanks, Steve. Thanks a lot."

Patient after patient who had read about what happened in the paper or had seen it on TV expressed their shock, disbelief, and support, then told me of my role in their families' lives. I told them as much as I thought I could about the situation, often way more than Kent would have been comfortable with, but I couldn't help it. I had cared for many of these people since I had been a resident. It was overwhelming at times that now they all wanted to help me.

I was back on track and beginning to hit my usual stride. God, I needed this; I needed to do this work. It was as therapeutic for me as it was for them.

There were a series of meetings with the hospital administration over a two week span. Bill Griffin, who entered the hospital's family practice residency as I was leaving it and now was its director, reviewed the files on which the government based the case. He found no evidence of fraud but thought I was "generous" in the amount of time off I gave for work-related injuries or conditions, and he saw deficiencies in my Evaluation and Management Coding skills. He was assigned to implement what was at first called a Personal Improvement Plan and then later labelled a disciplinary action to correct those problems.

E&M coding had actually been mandated by federal law in 1992 or so. I looked at it back then and immediately surmised that its potential to help me take better care of patients was zero. Its real purpose was to help insurance companies determine how little money they could get away with spending on the care of a patient. I hoped it would be dismissed as a bad idea before somebody made me fully comply with it. I was wrong. The time had come; I welcomed the assistance.

Ellen had made several attempts to get me to sit down with her and address the financial realities of the case. Each time, I got frustrated and upset and left her sitting at the table with the check book, her calculator, and a calendar. She finally cornered me.

"Nobody leaves this table until we at least figure out how we're going to pay Kent."

I actually had been thinking about it.

"For openers, let's take $6,000 from savings. Then, there should be at least that amount in my VA disability account."

"But that's your rainy day fund."

"Yeah, well, it's raining. Let's use that. Then let's get a home equity loan for as much as we can get on this place, then we cross our fingers. Let's hold off on a decision on selling until we can get a better idea how things are going to go."

I had caught her by surprise. She just looked at me for a few seconds before speaking.

"I'm impressed. That should work."

"Well, if you don't need me for anything else, I guess I'll go out back and watch the soybeans grow. Rudy, come on - let's go."

"Wait. I just believe this is all going to work out like it should, and we're going to be all right. Just hang in there, okay?"

"Okay, I'll try."

It wouldn't be easy. My past and the present were becoming harder to keep separate. Shortly, I'd be taking the money which the government was giving me for having been wounded while taking care of my people, and using it to help finance my legal defense against the same government, who now said I was a criminal for doing essentially the same thing. How could that not be okay?

On 8/14/99, I was arraigned in federal court in Detroit. It was an all-day event. Ellen was on her own while Kent and I began by checking in with a nice woman seated behind three-inch-thick bulletproof glass. Then we registered with a federal marshal seated at a desk opposite our chairs. Next, I got my mug shot taken and my fingerprints done. From there, it was down to a holding cell attended by two linebacker-types. They repeated the finger prints.

One asked the other: "Hey, do we need to put him in a holding cell? He's a doctor, for crying out loud?"

He responded: "Yeah, we do."

I was only in it for a couple minutes; I was set free for lunch. At a local deli, we brought Ellen up to speed on the morning's activities, and then we all went back for the actual arraignment.

We entered what looked like a huge courtroom and seated ourselves on one of many long benches. In the front, a robed female magistrate sat at a big elevated desk. I looked around the room as we awaited my turn. Two guys in orange jumpsuits with their wrists and ankles in chains were ahead of me.

When my case was called, Kent and I walked up and onto a large podium. The lady looked at some papers then down at me. I was ready to calmly explain my actions.

"Do you understand the charges brought against you?" She asked.

"Yes." I answered.

"How do you plead?"

"Not guilty."

She and Kent spoke briefly and determined that in lieu of bond, all I had to do was show up for the next round or have $50,000 worth of my assets seized. She signed some papers in front of her and then spoke to me.

"You're free to go."

Ellen and I knew that arraignment was not a trial, but I thought at some point in it I would have an opportunity to tell someone my side of the story. I just stood there. Kent gently closed his hand on my arm before the look on my face could be translated into speech. As he ushered me off the podium, Ellen met us in the aisle. On the way out, I turned to Kent.

"That's it. We're done?" I asked in disbelief.

"Yes. You did fine, Doctor." Kent answered.

We drove about thirty miles before Kent finally broke the silence.

"Doctor, you're very quiet. Are you all right?"

"Oh sure, Kent. I was just trying to remember if I'd ever been finger printed before, and I was. They did it just before we went into the field in Vietnam in case our heads were blown off."

It was quiet for another ten miles.

"Doctor, we need to talk about how you need to conduct yourself while this case is going on. Are you up to that?"

"Sure."

"Basically, you need to do anything anybody from the hospital asks you to do. Whether it sounds dumb, or whether you agree with it or not, you need to go along and keep a low profile. The more you can get them to say good things about you, the better it will look for your case. Any positive feedback given to you on paper I want you to fax to me. As you get progress reports on the improvement plan, I want them. I want you to stay out of any confrontations with any insurance companies, Medicare, patients, anybody! Do you understand what I mean?"

"Yeah; like when one of my patients comes in needing a new prosthetic leg and they've been getting jacked around for two months, I just tell them to keep calling the insurance company until they get what they need or their stump breaks down, right?"

"Exactly."

"You're serious, aren't you?"

"I am dead serious. You are in trouble, and that is how you got there. What makes you think that you have to do everything for these people, anyway? They're not even *your* patients anymore. They're Sparrow Health System's."

That hurt. I paused and then responded.

"You make it sound like some kind of character flaw, Kent."

"Maybe it is. You're way over the line on what you're willing to do for people. How did you get that way?"

"How did I get that way?"

I thought about telling him and decided this would be a good time to start in my new role.

"It wasn't easy, Kent."

On a beautiful night in September, we were standing on the deck. I had my arms around Ellen as she leaned back against my chest. The moon reflected off the pond. Stars filled the sky. Fireflies danced over the back thirty acres of soon-to-be-harvested soybeans.

"Rich?"

"Yeah?"

"You really impress me."

"Shucks, ma'am."

"No, I really mean that. I don't know anyone who would deal with what's happened the way you are. Those forms you've been working on are excellent, and your progress with coding is impressive."

"Thanks. You understand this stuff better than I ever will, so that really means a lot to me. I feel bad that it takes up so much time, and I know I haven't been easy to be around."

"You've got a lot on your plate."

It was quiet for a moment. Then she spoke.

"Tell me something."

"Yes, you can have me."

She elbowed me in the ribs.

"I'm serious."

"Okay, what?"

"Does anything ever scare you?"

There was a long silence.

"I don't like thinking about anything bad happening to you or any of the kids. I don't think I could come back from something like that."

"That makes me feel very special."

"You're my favorite person on the planet. I mean that objectively. I've met a lot of people, but no one quite like you. If anything happens to me, the only regret I'll have is that we didn't have more time together. I love you."

She turned. We kissed, softly and tenderly at first, then with more intensity.

"I love you, too."

We embraced longer.

"I've got to tuck Amanda in. When you come in, I'll tuck you in, too."

She slid the door open and went into the house. I walked across the deck, put my elbows on the rail, and stared off into the darkness.

Vietnam and home had one thing in common - the night. Right now, there were animals out there hunting each other, to kill or be killed. In Vietnam, we were all human beings doing the same thing. Having my wife in my arms on the deck in the dark was a good thing, but after she went in, I was alone. Past moments alone in the darkness were sometimes still a problem for me. Mortars raining down from nowhere were bad enough, but the cries of a dying woman I never saw and could not help were even worse. She was not a soldier or warrior for either side, I don't believe. She was a woman, probably a wife and mother, in pain, crying out, dying. Even though we spoke different languages, it was clear in the quality of her cries that her life was coming to an end, and I could do nothing but listen. I still hear her when I'm alone outside in the dark.

I raised myself from the deck railing and stood straight. I went back inside, up the stairs, and lay down on the bed. A few minutes later, Ellen came in and snuggled up. She kissed me in a fashion consistent with the mood out on the deck minutes before. I didn't reciprocate.

"I'm kind of tired. How about we just go to sleep," I said.

She gently moved away from me.

"It's okay, I understand." After a few moments of silence, she added, "It's not another woman, is it?"

I was struck by the irony of her question. Best keep it simple.

"No."

The first week of August, 1999, I got a registered letter in the office from Blue Cross saying I was being placed on something called Prior Payment Utilization Review. That meant I would have to submit complete documentation on every encounter with any of their insured before they would consider payment of the claim, and I would have to meet with the reviewers every six months.

This was for Ellen what a Code Blue would be for me. She understood the impact of PPUR far better than I did. The added work and the delay in payments could be the last straw for the hospital so far as my employment was concerned. That was probably its real purpose.

Kent and I talked on the phone the next day.

"I explained to the nice man who sent you that letter that you were already subject to a remedial program that was progressing to the satisfaction of your employer so that, in essence, what he's doing with PPUR is conducting a review of Sparrow Health System policy and procedures. It's unnecessarily punitive, and it seems like an unreasonable expenditure of resources for all concerned, but that's never bothered them in the past. It really shouldn't have been put in place, so I can't tell you how long we'll be dealing with it."

"So what do I do?"

"You do what you've always done: take good care of patients, keep working on the improvement plan with Doctor Griffin, try to keep your head up, and let the hospital deal with providing the requested data. Hopefully, the Blues will quickly tire of paying people to review your good work and get you off this."

There was a pause in the conversation.

"You okay, Doctor?"

I took in a long breath and exhaled slowly.

"I, ah," I paused. "I'm getting tired, Kent."

Kent paused about a millisecond.

"Buck up."

The first week of November 1999, I was called out of an exam room for a phone call.

"Doctor, you, Ellen, and I need to meet as soon as possible to discuss a new development in your case."

"Okay, Kent. When can you do it?"

"How about today after you finish seeing patients?"

"Uh oh. Can you give me a bit of an idea of what's up?"

"The U.S. Attorney is offering you a deal, a plea bargain."

"From the sound of your voice, I get the feeling that you're not real excited about it."

"Very perceptive as usual, Doctor. No, I'm not, and I don't think that you'll be either, but let's sit down the three of us and discuss it in person, and I'll give you the details then."

"I want you to look this over."

Kent slid a multipage document across the table to us.

"Take as much time as you need. We can go over it in as much detail as you might want, but, basically, what they're offering is that you plead guilty to a single count of mail fraud and lose your license to practice medicine in lieu of any jail time or fine."

Ellen finished first and spoke to Kent while I continued to read.

"They might as well shoot him," she said.

I looked up at her.

"That's what preventing him from practicing medicine will basically mean," she clarified.

I relaxed and put my head back down. She continued.

"What does this sound like to you, Kent?"

"In a nutshell?" he asked.

"Okay."

"Like, other than that, Mrs. Lincoln, how did you like the play?"

"Exactly. I say no way. Accepting this means he admits to having committed a crime. He hasn't. It would be wrong for him to say that he did. I say we fight this with everything we have, right, Rich?"

After a long silence, I responded.

"No."

"What?" Ellen was stunned. Kent was tougher to read, but he looked at least surprised.

"No," I repeated. "I can't put us through anymore of this. If it were just me, it would be a different story. This will just continue to drain more and more resources and opportunities away from the family, and to what end? So I can be a doctor and wait for some other institution to get a wild hair up its ass and do something else to us some other time? No, I don't think so. I think we've had enough."

"Don't say that," Ellen answered. "You didn't make those people sick or injure them. You diagnosed and treated them. Where in the hell do these people get off with this 'you cost them $160,000', and this 'much of which is suspected to be fraudulent' crap. And for this you'd give up your career? Don't worry about the resources; we'll find them. If we don't teach the kids one other thing, let it be that they should have the courage to stand up for themselves and what they believe in no matter what. That's what sharing my life with you has taught me."

We had completely reversed our usual roles. Ellen was ready to wage virtually unwinnable war. I was ready to accept defeat. No, I was actually surrendering. We were both surprised at what we had just heard each other say. Kent broke the silence that followed.

"We don't have to reach a decision on this tonight. We have a few days."

I could see their eyes were on me, despite me looking at the floor.

"Would you like to go through this in any greater detail and-"

I lifted my head and looked at him.

"No. Just give me a few minutes."

I was overwhelmed. I hoped and believed that after Kent informed the U.S. Attorney's office that I was not self-employed, they would take a closer look at the case. Also, Kent had sent them a copy of the "The President and Some of My Other Friends" early on to provide insight into my actions at the investigator's second visit. He knew that one of the men involved in the investigation was a Vietnam veteran who might understand. Obviously, I was wrong.

There were thirteen defendants in this statewide sting operation: twelve of whom did what they were accused of, and one who didn't. Essentially, I was just collateral damage like the kids at Third Field. I could see their faces: the napalm girls and the kids from the school bus. They had inspired me to go on, not as a warrior, but as a human being.

Since then, as a doctor, I had done a lot of good for a lot of people, and I could do more. I had to do more because somehow for me, doing so made the war experiences a positive motivating force in my life instead of something that could ruin it. That was my ongoing battle and I feared the consequences of being prevented from fighting it, especially for this reason.

Kent and Ellen had been talking, but I hadn't been listening. I tossed the papers back on the table.

"*Okay*," I announced in a voice that must have been louder than necessary.

They stopped talking and looked at me.

"I think I have this in better perspective now."

"We have until the nineteenth of the month to respond, Doctor."

"No, I don't need any more time, Kent. Do you think that you could find some nice legal and corporately correct way to tell these people to go fuck themselves?"

"Amen! That's better, Rich." Ellen was relieved.

"I think I can polish that up a tad without losing the clarity, Doctor."

"And tell them that <u>The United States of America vs. Richard Czop</u> is not a fair fight. They'd better get Canada and Mexico on board, too."

CHAPTER 11

Christmas was the best and most important time of the year for Ellen. It was all about love and joy and family. The decorations – Hallmark Villages, snow babies, lights, garland – always went up inside the house the day after Thanksgiving.

After the U. S. Attorney asserted his intention to end my career, I had to surrender any hope or delusion I had that the Department of Justice would decide a mistake had been made in charging me. The evidence to justify his position was in the seventeen charts the FBI had seized. They returned copies of them to me shortly after the raid on the office. I had glanced at them a few times, but not with the careful scrutiny that was now necessary to prepare a defense. I had the weekend off, and I sentenced myself to spend it at my desk in the basement. Maybe I had made mistakes.

I started with those who had the most absences. First was a man who was probably off for minor problems more than he was working. Multiple requests to his supervisor to contact me were documented; no response was ever received. There was a copy of a letter I sent to the patient suggesting he either find a doctor who could keep him healthier, or find a way to work despite minor ailments.

The next was a patient I had restricted from working in the paint booth because of severe asthma. A doctor from GM Medical called and informed me that he was "overriding" my restriction. Despite telling him and documenting in the chart that I thought doing so would constitute battery, he did it. She promptly developed an asthma attack that required hospital admission. I called the head of GM medical about the incident, and the physician in question was fired.

If these two were the worst of the lot, I didn't need to look at any more. Maybe the move out to the country on a 56-acre property while under investigation for fraudulently obtaining money was part of it. My father was an electrician; my mother a grocery store cashier. Both had worked hard to accomplish the only goals in life that I had ever heard either of them express: to raise good sons and give them opportunities in life that they themselves had never had. Both died comfortable in the knowledge that they had accomplished what they had set out to do. It was money left me by my parents that made the move to the country possible, not stealing from General Motors.

I hadn't spent much time looking at the reports the investigator had submitted detailing what had transpired between us at his two visits. I tried, but I just couldn't do it. I thought it was because they made me look like a criminal and sound like a fool. I felt embarrassed and angry. Today, I had to get past that because they were at the heart of this whole ugly affair. I had to remember every detail and work through this, no matter how it made me feel.

The first one took place on June 24, 1997. The wire he wore reportedly "malfunctioned", so there was no transcription of recorded conversation for it, only my typed chart note documenting the encounter. I reviewed it, and it triggered my recollection of more information about the visit.

Sharon, my medical assistant, had vibes about him which she shared before I entered the room.

"I need to talk to you about this next one," she said.

"Okay."

"He's weird. He's a new patient, and he wants you to cover him for being off work golfing. There's just something not right about the guy."

"Is it my imagination or is this place getting a little more bizarre every day?" I asked.

"It sure is. This one seems to be a little ways out there."

Sharon is good. The guy made her uncomfortable. I had been directed by the hospital administration to open my practice and start taking new patients to enhance income generation. I didn't want to because this is the kind of stuff you have to deal with, i.e. deadbeats, drug seekers, the incurable non-ill, etc. I'd listen, and then I'd most likely throw him out.

"What can I do for you?" I asked as I entered the room.

I didn't introduce myself, and I did not go out of my way to be warm or friendly. I didn't need this kind of individual as a patient, no matter what the hospital said.

"I need a work slip. I called in sick when I was actually up North playing golf."

I looked at him. He seemed nervous and embarrassed by what he had just said. After a moment, I spoke.

"Well, at least you're honest. You should hear some of the stories people tell me."

He had caught me off guard. Cheats and malingerers don't usually tell the truth, but people who are in distress and need help usually do.

"I have a lot of stress," he added.

"Yeah, I'm sure that golf could cause stress and require you to take time off work," I sarcastically responded.

I wasn't ready to warm up to this individual. He was a new patient, and we had to start a chart on him. He had filled out our forms, and I began to silently read what he had written down.

"You had a twenty year marriage that ended in divorce?"

"Yes."

"And there was a child involved. Was that a son or a daughter?"

"I have a son."

I paused and looked at him.

"That must have been tough."

"Very tough," he answered. His eyes seemed to moisten and he looked away.

My divorce was one of the most difficult experiences of my life, and I remembered how it felt to live alone in an apartment after having a home and living with my family.

"What does your job as 'Assembly – Relief' entail?" I asked.

"I work on the assembly line in an auto plant."

"It says you've been doing that for twenty-two years."

"Yes."

"Are you guys still on twelve hour shifts?" I asked.

"Yes," he answered.

I worked in factories during summers in high school and college. It was mind-numbing, and I only had to do it for a few months. It was time to lighten up on this guy. He was being pounded. I looked at him.

"Ya know what, I can't hit a straight drive to save my ass."

The guy looked like the weight of the world had been lifted off of him. He started telling me about a good local pro who had given him some lessons. Then he began to talk more freely about being under significant stress, and that was why he had to get out even though he had no time off available. I thought there were a lot worse choices he could have made.

He wasn't boasting about what he had done; he seemed contrite. I had no reason to doubt he was telling the truth. It seemed he realized that he had done wrong and was in trouble as a result. I decided to take him on as a new patient. He needed to be given a break.

"I'm going to cover you. But in the future, I want you to come in when things start piling up on you, not when you can't stand it anymore. We'll do whatever we need to do so that you don't have to pull something like this again. I'm going put this down as situational stress."

"Gee, thanks Doc. I really appreciate this."

The reason the wire "malfunctioned" at the visit was obvious.

"What did you do with that guy?" Sharon asked after the patient left.

"I took him on and covered him. He got stressed out. I think we can help him."

I moved on to the second encounter, which took place on January 29, 1999. I started reading the transcript, studying every word as if it was a cell under a microscope.

My initial words to him when I entered the room sounded like I was happy to see him. That was because I thought he was someone else - ironically, a Lansing Police detective with whom I had had infrequent but very positive encounters over many years. Usually they centered on an annual debate of the pros and cons of injecting his right shoulder with cortisone to allow him another season of basketball in his late fifties. There was even a striking physical resemblance.

"I ah, gave your nurse an excuse. I called in sick this morning. I want to go south with some buddies and play golf, and GM won't give us any time off, so I want to call in sick for a week, and I-I gave your nurse an excuse. I didn't... I want to go down to South Carolina and play for a week."

I looked in his chart and realized who I was actually dealing with and quickly reoriented. This wasn't a friend. This was someone who I had previously given the benefit of the doubt as being honest, in trouble, and in need of help. I could deal with having been wrong and taken advantage of, but to have him think that he could do it again, now that pissed me off. My first reaction was to throw him out, but his demeanor had changed since the first encounter.

"There's absolutely nothing wrong with me," he announced in a louder-than-necessary volume while he leaned back against the wall, extended his legs out straight, and raised both arms over his head. Gone was the beaten down, embarrassed, apologetic demeanor of the first encounter. His new expression was arrogant and his body language more animated, suggesting a potential for aggression. Throwing him out no longer sounded like a safe plan.

I cautiously proceeded to try to determine exactly what I was dealing with.

I looked back down into his chart. I decided to read aloud part of the note for his first visit. I wanted to both hear and see his response.

"I'm impressed with his honesty. I don't know him well. If he comes in next week needing coverage for more time off, my recommendation is going to change, otherwise I can, in clear conscience, cover him for what he's asking."

I was telling him that I had believed what he told me, trusted him, and even went out on a limb for him. Those statements would cry out for a response from a normal, rational person; something along the lines of an apology or explanation. I remembered looking up at him and waiting.

"It felt real good last time, Doctor," he answered with a cocky smirk on his face.

That was not the response I was hoping for.

"There's absolutely nothing wrong with me," he repeated. "I lied to the receptionist to get on the schedule. I just want a week off to play golf."

The transcript did not contain the words with which he ended that statement, but I have absolutely no doubt that he said, "…and you're going to cover me for it."

His words and unsettling body language were "red flags." There were others. Coming to a physician and stating "there is absolutely nothing wrong," outside the context of a screening physical examination or a recheck after an illness, is inherently bizarre. In addition, a malingerer would have said he was sick in order to get time off, and he would do it often. This guy said he was fine, and he had had no contact with the office – in person, by phone, or by letter – in the 18 months between visits.

I made my diagnosis: he was a sociopath. I was lucky last time, but now he was clearly more desperate and he could be dangerous. Neither police nor commitment options were realistic. He had not broken any laws, and he was not psychotic. I decided to say whatever I needed to say, do whatever I needed to do, just get him the hell out of here and out his workplace. It was best I not touch his stress or the potential sources of it with a ten-foot pole. Not today. Above all, don't piss him off. Identify with him; find common ground. It was golf before.

Thus began a few minutes of brainless banter about golf, in the midst of which, I told him I would cover him.

"You are going to have to tell me something different than this, though. I can't put the reason down as playing golf. You'll have to lie," I said to him. I didn't suspect he'd have a problem with that. Under the circumstances, I didn't.

"M-M-M-My back bothers a lot, yeah, and – and I do have problems shoveling snow. I have that kind of problem, lower back pain, that's the problem," he said.

I had him sit on the exam table and checked his lower extremity reflexes as I would for a legitimate spine complaint. I wanted to keep this looking to him as much like a typical medical encounter as I could. I told him that he could get off the table and have a seat. I sat down, rolled the wheeled examining stool to the table, and started to write a note for the visit.

"I'm going to say that you are having a flare-up of a chronic lower back problem."

It looked like I was home free. Then he said something else that does not appear in the transcript but which I will never forget.

"I really need this, and you're the only thing standing in my way."

I stopped writing, but I kept looking down at the chart. He did not need to make a statement like that. I had already told him that I was going to cover him. My back had been to him. I knew this was trouble; I turned to face him. He was out of the chair, standing midway between the door and the exam stool. I was looking up at him. He was dressed completely in black. I shook my pen, pretending it ran out of ink and went to a cabinet drawer as if to get another. Scalpels had recently been removed from exam rooms for patient safety. I hoped one might have been missed. If so, I would slide it up my sleeve and use it to fight my way out if he pulled a weapon or made a threatening move toward me.

As clear and complete as my recollection of my encounters with this man had been, I have absolutely no idea about what transpired between the moment I turned from the cabinet drawer to face him and the conclusion of the encounter which actually occurred in the hallway. I kept talking to him; I said when he got back, he needed to arrange a physical with lab tests and a chest x-ray in order for me to thoroughly assess him.

"If you want to still be playing golf when you are eighty years old, we need to start planning your care now." I added.

There is absolutely no doubt in my mind that I said that to him, but, once again, those words did not appear in the transcript of his recording. Then I went up to the reception area and pretended to be looking for a chart while he checked out. I wanted to make sure that he exited the office without incident.

When he was gone, I told the staff, "That guy just came in here and asked me for a week off to play golf, and I gave it to him. I can't believe that. I give up. I've had it with this bullshit."

They could see I was upset, but nobody quite knew what to say. I needed some time to think about what had just happened, but there was none. I went into my office, where I pulled out my "reminder file." I removed the card for two months down the road. That would be plenty of time for him to have arranged the physical I had advised. If he hadn't by then, I would have my excuse to discharge him from the practice. I had my pen in hand and the card on the desk, but I couldn't bring myself to make that entry. I never wanted to lay eyes on this guy again.

I stood up and pushed the chair under the desk with enough force that Rudy, who had been sleeping next to it, sprang to his feet. I walked over to the sliding glass door and looked out back. I wanted to take Rudy and go out and run at full speed until I dropped. Then I decided that I needed to finish this. I had objectively reconstructed the whole case; I knew what I had done and why. I had to get past the emotion and keep control. I sat back down at the desk.

Blue Cross believed that this was going to be a simple, straightforward, often repeated scenario, wherein I would sit there and hand the investigator a time-off slip and he would hand me money. They got it totally wrong. First, I was honest, I was not self-employed, and my employer monitored my financial productivity on a per visit basis down to the penny. In legal terms, I lacked motive, means, or opportunity to have done what they accused me of. Second, they demonstrated at the very least, poor insight, and at worst, blatant ignorance, of the dynamics of the doctor-patient encounter in the family practice setting. Third, they made the decision to proceed with prosecution based on tainted evidence obtained from two flagrantly flawed encounters with an undercover investigator.

In the process, they created for me, as a veteran of guerilla warfare in Vietnam with problems dealing with subsequent PTSD, a perfect storm. I had been put face to face with a man taller than me, dressed in black from head to toe, who was masquerading as something he was not. In Vietnam, people like that killed American soldiers. Was his uniform today part of the plan? I had worked for Blue Cross, and they knew from my resume that I was a Vietnam veteran. One of the men who worked on bringing the case was the Vietnam veteran Kent sent my book to. I had to repress that thought; if I let myself believe it, I would have to do something about it.

I had, based on certain behaviors he demonstrated and features of the setting, perceived a life-threatening risk to myself and my staff if this individual chose to or was provoked to act. I was weaponless, unprotected, and in a vulnerable position. I had turned my back on someone. I had left myself with no way out. I prepared to take his life before he took mine. I was put in that position by the U. S. government. If I could not save my own life, maybe I could make it possible for others who were in the area to escape.

Was this my office or Vietnam? It was both. Welcome to my world.

"Are you going to put up some lights outside?"

I hadn't heard Ellen come down the steps. I came two inches out of my chair.

"I didn't mean to startle you," she apologized.

"It's okay," I answered

"It doesn't have to be much; just a little something to brighten up the house. It might help you to get into the Christmas spirit a little bit."

I looked at her face and into her eyes.

"I want to; I just can't do it right now."

She put her hands on my shoulders and rubbed my neck.

"You're all sweaty. Are you coming down with something? Do you want me to get you a couple Tylenol?"

"No, I'm okay. Thanks anyway. I'm just in kind of a bad place right now."

"I know. We all are. But let's not let them ruin the holidays for us."

Too late.

CHAPTER 12

The lights never did get put up, and on Christmas Eve, after two bad weeks of alternating arguments and silence, I left. I had been driving for nearly two hours with no thought as to direction or destination. Nothing had really registered with me until a road sign that I hadn't seen in years appeared: Highway 421, exit one mile. Sixty-five miles to the south was St. Joseph's College. I had done my freshman year of college at St. Joe's before transferring to Michigan State. Now, it seemed like a lifetime ago. Actually, it was. Over the years, I had thought about going back to see the place sometime, but I had never gotten around to it. I took the exit.

After an hour, I could see the old water tower and the chapel steeple in the distance. Ten minutes later, I turned into the main entrance. I didn't even park; I just let the car roll to a stop, shut it off, and got out.

From where I stood, I could see pretty much the entire campus. It was completely still: silent, no traffic, not a living soul in sight. Everyone had gone home to be with their loved ones for Christmas. I had left mine and come to this tiny, isolated, closed college.

I started to look around. Except for the obvious absence of the old administration building, which was already ancient when I attended classes here, the place was completely unchanged. I looked at what were then the two most important buildings in my life - the chapel and the post office. There was my dorm, and for a second, I could almost smell fresh popcorn and hear "Like a Rolling Stone" playing on a stereo somewhere. Turning toward town, I saw the field house, the site of the most memorable moment of the year - Judy Collins performing in concert at the Spring Festival of 1966.

The last time I had stood on this spot, I was a nineteen year-old kid afraid, to say that he was in pre-med until getting the kind of grades that would back it up. I didn't have much time to think about the world. I was too busy studying and being homesick. I had to call home at least twice a week to be reassured and encouraged by my mother and father.

That same year, Tom was a freshman in pre-dent at Aquinas College in Grand Rapids. There was no way back then for either of us to see what waited just around the bend in the road of our lives, but it didn't matter, because we were ready, and we knew the rules: "thou shalt not this" and "thou shalt that." We knew all about love, the greatest measure of which was "to lay down one's life for a friend." What else did we need to know?

Then it all seemed to come unraveled. Tom went to the war and came home quadriplegic. I went. Then they just kind of stopped having the war and North and South Vietnam reunited. We will never know what the more than 58,000 American soldiers killed there might have thought about that.

I did another slow 360, studying the place as I turned. I thought about taking a walk over to the chapel, but I decided it would probably be locked. Just as well; my faith was another casualty of the war.

I leaned back against the side of the car and waited for some kind of "vision" or other miraculous event to occur. Maybe Jesus or His Mom would appear and tell me that I was still a good boy, dust me off a little, and send me back to my life restored, renewed, re-inspired. I had to settle for a simple insight.

I came to the sudden realization that I had actually achieved everything that I had worked and prayed so hard for while a student here. I was a good physician, and many of my patients cared as much about me as I did about them. I had a wife I loved and who loved me and who would do whatever she had to do to protect our family against anything or anybody who threatened it, even if it was me. I was the father of good children who were still in need of my reassurance, support, and direction. None of that would have happened if I had been killed in Vietnam, but I wasn't.

I took one last look around, then got back in the car and headed out the front drive. I didn't look back.

It was 10:30 p.m. when the cell phone rang. It was Ellen.
"I just wanted to make sure you were alright."
"Thanks. I'm okay.
"Where are you?"
"I'm just about back. I took a ride down to St. Joe's in Indiana."
"You always wanted to do that. How was it?"
"I think it helped. Can I come home… please?"
"If that's what you really want."
"Do you want me to?"
Ellen always tells the truth.
"I don't know."

I knew that the "I'm sorry" I said to everybody when I got home wouldn't undo the damage I had done or the shame I felt. It was still Christmas Eve, but nobody quite knew what to do.
"Why don't we just open presents and try to make the best of it," Ellen offered.
That's what we did. She handed me a small package.
"I hope you don't take this wrong."
I opened it. It was a videocassette, <u>Enemy of the State</u> with Will Smith.
"It's perfect. Thank you."
She hugged me and gave me a kiss.

The following morning, I was sitting on the side of the bed when

Ellen woke up and sat up next to me.

"Rich, we need to talk."

"Yeah, I know."

"I don't think you appreciate the strain that you're under."

"I can handle it."

"We can't. Everybody's afraid. You get mad easily. You hurt people by what you say, and you expect everybody to accept that. That's no way to live. I've let it go too long. Now you look like you could hurt people physically. I'm not going to let that happen. You've got to get help."

"I think you're making a bigger deal out of this stuff than it really is."

"No," she calmly answered. "I'm not."

Ellen never really had a childhood. He father died of lung cancer in his early forties when she was just seven. She took on adult responsibilities when she should have been playing kid games. Her mother remarried, and alcohol and physical abuse were commonplace in the new marriage. Ellen saw it, protected her mother from it as best she could, and promised herself she would never tolerate that kind of treatment from anyone.

It was New Year's Eve. A new millennium was about to begin. Everyone else was excited.

"Are you going to get ready soon?" Ellen asked as I laid on the couch.

"Yeah, I'll take a quick shower and shave. It won't take me long."

"Good. We're looking forward to this. It'll be good to see everybody again."

Our old next door neighbors were throwing a party. There'd be food, a DJ, and friends. I had not been with these people since becoming an alleged federal felon. They would want to know what happened, and I wouldn't be at liberty to tell them, and even if I could, I was tired of hearing myself say it. Among the group would be the realtor who had beautifully coordinated the sale of our old house and the acquisition of my "dream property," which we would probably lose in the not too distant future.

"Yeah, it should be fun," I mumbled as I got up and headed upstairs.

I had yet to share with Ellen the numbers for business-done at the office in December. Despite working hard all month and raising the total $5,000 over the previous month, I finished $400 below the target, the one based on no time off. I had done everything I could do, short of donning a clown suit and waving people in off the street with a towel, and I had still come up short.

When I came back down, Ellen looked at me for a few seconds.

"Are you going to be able to cheer up and have some fun?"

I didn't say anything. I just stood there thinking about how I might do that. Then I answered, "No, I don't think I am."

"Are you sure?"

"Yeah, I am, but you guys go."

"Okay. Do you want us to call you at midnight?"

"No, I'm just going to go to bed and end this year as soon as I can."

The first day of 2000 was gray with a fog-like mist. After lunch, Ellen and the girls went into town to see a "chick flick." They had said that the party was great and that everybody there said to say "hi" to me and tell me that they were sorry I couldn't make it, but that they understood. I wish I did. All I knew was that I was in trouble, and that I had to snap out of this.

"Rudy! Want to go for a ride in the Bronco?"

Nothing made him go more nuts than those words. Riding around the back forty with a dog in a beat-up old truck usually worked for me when things were bad, but they had never been this bad. We headed out to the pole barn and slid open the huge sliding doors at the north end. There sat the twenty-one year-old Bronco I bought for plowing the drive way. Everything but the windows and headlights were painted flat black. I opened the driver's side door. Rudy jumped in, and I followed. Inside, there were two bucket seats and nothing else. There was a hole with wires visible where the glove box had been, and more wires hung down from several places below the dashboard. The only gauges that worked were fuel and temperature. It looked like a grenade had gone off inside it. Nobody else wanted to sit in the Bronco, much less ride in it.

I pumped the accelerator a few times, turned the key, and the monster roared to life. Without a muffler and inside the pole barn, it sounded awesome. I backed it out. To complete the process of putting it into 4-wheel drive, I got out and locked the front wheel hubs. We were ready. I stepped on the gas and aimed it down the dirt road along the east fence line, bouncing and swerving all the way down to the river.

We got out, and Rudy started running in and out of the brush like he was in dog heaven while I walked in the woods along the riverbank. Usually all this was fun, but today it wasn't. Nothing was fun anymore. Nothing that I did seemed to do what I intended. For the second time in my life, after thirteen years of marriage, the possibility of divorce loomed. I felt that I could handle whatever pressure the outside world might bring to bear on me as long as "home" was safe and secure, but it wasn't anymore, thanks to me. I kept getting this feeling like I was being held under water, and I couldn't break free of the grasp on me, and I couldn't hold my breath much longer.

We had walked almost an hour and were now back to where we had left the Bronco. There was a small point of land that jutted out into the river. There was a tree on it, and when standing at its base you could turn around and see the house up the hill through an opening between branches. It was one of my favorite places on earth. As I stood there, I began to think how good it would be to just hang around there; then, just hang there; then, from that tree; from that thin cable in the truck. No more pain for me or for anyone.

I turned, ran back to the truck, and swung open the door. Rudy jumped in, and then I followed. I was sweating and breathing fast. I'm not sure how long we sat there. Then, with a turn of the key, the Bronco roared back to life.

"Fuck you!" I yelled out. "You don't get me; not then, not now. You don't get mine - not ever." We fishtailed and sprayed mud all the way up the hill back to the barn.

CHAPTER 13

When I got home from my first day at work in the new millennium, Ellen was at the door.

"Everything go okay?"

"Yeah, it was hectic but doable. By the way, I made an appointment with Jim Gowens for this Thursday. Will you go with me?"

"Sure." She paused and smiled at me. "Rich, thank you."

Jim is a family and child therapist whom we had initially used for help with issues surrounding ex-spouses and joint custody. After one visit with us, he decided it would be most useful to see me individually.

The sequence of events that led to the end of my first marriage was repeating itself because I didn't do anything different to prevent it from happening again. Only the names changed because I refused to. Janine became Ellen, Kathleen and Meegan became Amy and Amanda, and Jon McKindry became Jim Gowens. The Vietnam War became the <u>UNITED STATES v RICHARD CZOP</u>.

By mid-March, life had stabilized somewhat. I had met the requirements of the personal improvement plan with Bill Griffin's help, and my total charges were very close to the numbers needed to keep my job, so the hospital was happy. The Department of Justice was silent, leading me to hope that maybe someone had re-thought this whole matter and saw it for what it was. Working with Dr. Gowens was as helpful as it could be with my unwillingness to admit the role PTSD was playing in my life. On a Friday night, Ellen and I found ourselves with an empty house, and when dinner was over, we sat down to take a serious look at where we were.

"Ellen, I think we need to sell the house."

She dropped her pen. We had discussed selling the house the day the FBI had shown up but not since. She saw me as getting hammered from all directions and the place was the only thing holding me together.

The move had been hard on everyone else; she had just been waiting for the right time and the right way to bring it up.

"Are you sure? Could you do that?" She asked.

"Yeah. I totally underestimated how hard moving out here would be on everybody else. Amanda used to run across the street and play for a half hour. Now it's a sixty minute round trip by car to do that, and she doesn't want to make more work for us, so she spends most of the time alone. Amy's crowd makes decisions on hanging out or partying on the spur of the moment and changes them faster than that. First she's got to find them, and then she's got to leave for home a half-hour early and drive a long way on country roads in a hurry while pissed. We need to sell it before we're forced to, and we need to get back as close as we can to where we were and plug the kids back into their old lives."

Ellen's eyes moistened; she was physically and emotionally drained. She looked like she was being lifted out of a pit. We stood and embraced. Her cheek was wet.

"You really are unbelievable, do you know that?" she said.

"The only thing unbelievable about me is that you people haven't given up on me."

The following Monday, I saw a couple in the office who were familiar with my situation and mentioned having to sell. They came and looked, fell in love with the place and bought it.

On May 2, 2000 at 9 a.m., we closed on the sale of the farm. At 3 p.m., we closed on a house approximately 100 yards from the one we had left just over a year ago. Our new place was vacant, so within ten days of closing, Ellen and I were packing the last of the leftover awkward junk from the pole barn into the van. After a few tries, the tailgate finally compacted it all enough to latch.

"Do you feel like taking a last walk around?" I asked Ellen.

"Sure."

I took her hand, and we headed out back into the secret and beautiful place that people driving by on the road out front had no clue existed. After a few minutes, I asked her how she felt. She responded deliberately and only after deep reflection, like always.

"I'm grateful for the good times we've had here and grateful, in some ways, that we're leaving."

I didn't say anything for once. She continued.

"We've been through a lot, and I think we're all better people because we were able to do that. But I guess more than anything, I feel bitter. You're a great doctor. You've always gone out of your way to be fair and honest. We have worked so hard. This is totally wrong. There was no reason for them to do this to you and to us. It's got to be worse for you. Aren't you bitter about it?"

"I keep trying to think positive, but it isn't easy. Every day, I struggle with bureaucratic bullshit that only makes it harder to render good care. Every day, I have to jump through hoops to make it easier for insurance companies to take worse care of patients. And *I'm* the fucking criminal in all this?"

"I know. I feel the same way," Ellen added.

I started in again.

"Out here, it was like our own little world, and everything made sense. I could fish when I wanted to, in or out of season, with or without a license. The only rule was to maintain a balance between how many fish were taken out and how fast the others could reproduce. I could drive the Bronco on the property without a license in my pocket, plates on it, or even a damn road. It was all about being alive and being free."

We walked in silence for a short way.

"I'll tell you something else that you don't know about."

"What's that?" she answered.

"Walking in these woods, for the first time since Vietnam, I found myself looking at the ground for animal tracks and traces instead of trip wires and punji pits. If something moved in the brush, I was beginning to think animal instead of ambush."

She stopped and looked at me.

"Why didn't you tell me that before?"

"It's not something that I wanted you to know."

We walked on in silence for a while to the edge of what was now an early wheat field. Beneath our feet was what we used to call dirt, but now we knew it as soil, fertile soil, forty acres of which we leased to a local farmer who worked it. We had watched like kids at a circus as the seeds that he planted sprouted and over a few months evolved into a beautiful, healthy crop of soybeans. At harvest time, he let us ride with him in the combine that turned our yard into food. The very next day, he fertilized and drilled, not planted, wheat. It would have been nice to see it mature and wave in the breeze, our own personal amber wave of grain.

As we walked the grassy path that divided the woods near the house, four deer ran out and crossed the wheat field in about six seconds flat.

"Yep, the food chain is real," I said. Ellen had heard me say that enough to go ahead and finish it for me.

"And it's damn good to be at the top of it."

Thirty-one deer in view at one time was the record, but small groups came around every day, often right up to the salt block that we had put out for them near the house. From the deck after dark with a hand-held spotlight, we could see their luminescent eyes, as well as those of raccoon, skunk, and coyote, all moving silently about, on the lookout for something smaller to eat or something bigger to not be eaten by. If a deer went down, there'd be nothing left but a skeleton within a week.

We walked up a small rise, and there was the pond - our favorite thing. It was clean, spring-fed, two-and-a-half acres in surface area and fifteen feet at its deepest point. We could fish it, swim in it, row the twenty-five year-old flat bottom boat on it, or just look at it and the wildlife that it attracted. We had chosen the smallest of the house's three bedrooms for ours because it overlooked the pond.

"What's your best memory of living here?" I asked Ellen as we turned and headed back up to the house.

She walked a few feet in silence and deep thought before a smile came to her face and she answered.

"I'll never forget watching Amanda driving that old golf cart with Rudy sitting there next to her."

She started to laugh as her gaze traced their favorite route from the house down to the pond.

"I can still see the sun on their faces and the wind blowing her hair and his ears straight back as she drove around with him. That would have to be it for me. What is yours?"

I had to turn away and walk a few steps before I could respond: "your face as you were saying that."

Amy was back in the old neighborhood and re-synchronized her watch with her friends. Her life got easier immediately. Ellen and Amanda would have some overlap with our life in Charlotte for a month while the school year came to an end, but there was some instant improvement in both their lives. The only visible reminder of the farm was the old truck in the driveway.

The Bronco was my last link to the farm. I bought it for its snowplow after the first time I got stuck coming up the driveway. We couldn't have lived there without it. On Sundays, Rudy and I would drive the couple miles to The Country Store to buy a newspaper and a pack of Twinkies. On the way home I would eat one and feed him the other. When we got there we would drive to the back of the property and watch and listen to the Thornapple River run by. We were the essence of most country songs ever written. Seeing the Bronco in the driveway back in Lansing was like watching a fish try to live on land. I sold it.

Shortly after, I learned something that made the case even more hateful to me. When the charges were first brought and the complaint paperwork revealed the identity of the investigator, Ellen immediately recognized the name.

"Remember your first nurse?" she had asked me at the time.

"You mean Jan Barkley? Yeah, of course, I do."

"Well, this was her daughter's married name, and if I'm not mistaken, her husband was a Lansing cop."

When she told me that, it hurt too much to think that there might be any possible connection between someone I cherished as a dear and longtime friend and the investigator. I did not pursue it. Now, for some reason, I had to know.

"I called Jan Barkley today, and you were right: the undercover investigator was her daughter's husband, but they divorced a long time ago. We had a nice chat. She didn't know."

"That's really sick."

"What's sick about it? He's a cop. That's what they do."

"Don't you remember?"

"What? I don't think I ever met the guy. Did I?"

"No, you never met him, but you met his wife."

"I did? When?"

"Right after you went into practice. Jan's grandson was less than a year old and was sick. Nothing that they were being told to do by their doctor seemed to be helping, and her daughter felt like she wasn't being listened to, so Jan asked you to take a look at him."

"Oh yeah, I remember that, he was clearly failing to thrive and features of malabsorption were obvious. I worked him up and diagnosed celiac disease at about eight months of age, put him on the appropriate diet, and he turned right around. Then I hooked them up with Mr. Pediatrics for continuing care."

Dan Knickerson was one of my preceptors in medical school and residency. He was a great doctor, human being, and above all, friend.

"I remember Knick was so proud of me. He said I saved the kid and probably the family, too, and I thanked him for teaching me which end of a baby the food goes in."

For the first time in a while, I felt a smile on my face.

"I had forgotten all about that. That kid should have lived happily ever after," I added.

"Well, it took almost twenty years, but you finally met his Daddy."

The smile faded.

Amy's high school graduation, the most important day in her life to that point, would be the next big event I would let my bitterness and resentment ruin. After a loud and threatening verbal outburst at Ellen, I did not attend the ceremony. When they left the house to go to it, I left, too.

For the second time in six months, I felt the same need and/or compulsion to get away, to escape, but this time, I was shackled by being on call for five physicians, so I could not go far. I checked into the Kellogg Center, Michigan State University's Hotel and Conference Center. Waverly High School's graduation ceremony was actually taking place across the campus at MSU's Wharton Center for the Performing Arts. In some strange way, it was almost like I could still be a part of things by being in this place.

I sat on the side of the bed for a few moments staring at nothing in particular; I got up and opened the curtains. Outside was Brody Dormitory Complex, where I had lived for two years after transferring from St. Joe's after my freshman year ended. Once again, I was isolated and looking at a landscape from my past that was virtually unchanged, just like St. Joseph's last Christmas Eve. I watched people walking to and from places I had walked. It was like I was looking for myself in a better time.

Something was drastically wrong with me. For the second time in six months, I found myself in more pain than I could stand. I looked at the clock. I could still make it to Home Depot. I calculated the length of dryer vent tubing it would take to reach from the car's exhaust pipe to the side window. I wouldn't need a garage. I could just go someplace peaceful.

"Like you haven't done enough damage already today," I heard myself say out loud.

I went back home two nights later, and Ellen asked me to please leave. For the first time, I broke down so violently that she was afraid of what would happen if I left, so she let me stay.

Jim Gowens listened without speaking or changing his facial expression while I told him everything that had gone on surrounding Amy's graduation. There was silence after I finished talking. Then he spoke.

"Rich, I think you should try an SSRI."

The selective serotonin reuptake inhibitors are a class of medicines that affect certain substances in the brain called neurotransmitters, alterations of which are believed to underlie depression and some other mood disorders.

"I don't think I'm depressed."

"I suspect that you are to some degree, but you know that they are not just anti-depressants. They have effects on anger management, and there is data to support their benefit to people suffering from Post-Traumatic Stress Disorder. I think it would be a good idea or at least worth a try."

I shook my head and half smiled.

"Good old PTSD. I wondered when you were going to get around to that."

"I've tried before, but you do not seem able to accept it. I think it's playing a major role here."

"Well, you're not alone. The psychologist we saw when the first marriage broke up did, too."

"And you don't think so?"

"Okay, okay, I admit it, I'm fucked up. There, is that what you want me to say?"

Jim did not respond at first. I just looked down at the floor.

"It was hell, Rich. Why you went, how long or short you stayed, or why you survived is irrelevant. You don't owe anything to anyone who didn't, or who was there longer, or was more physically or mentally damaged. The only people you owe anything to are your family. You owe them you; you living in their time and place."

I sat back and directed my gaze from the floor to the ceiling. I thought long and hard about what he had just said.

"I think it's too late, Jim. I at the bottom of a hole I dug, and I'm being buried alive in it."

Jim took a long time to answer.

"Rich, do you see what's happening? You are reliving your worst fear. There's a battle raging around you, you are powerless, and you are hoping to die before you have to watch yourself be killed."

After a few seconds of processing, I was able to respond: "Oh, my God…"

"Give yourself a chance, Rich. In your own way today, you admitted for the first time that you have a problem, and you're taking responsibility for it. That's a major step. You need to buy yourself some time. You don't have anything to lose by trying a medication."

It's supposed to take a week or two for the effect of an SSRI to become apparent. I could feel a positive change in 48 hours. Within a week, it was obvious to everyone close to me. I was easier to live with. I rested well, and thoughts of violence were rare and fleeting.

On June 29, 2000, the hospital sent a new one year contract to the office for my signature.

We had been given some time to heal.

In November 2000, Kent called me.

"Doctor, if I'm not mistaken, you're either about to or have recently had your next meeting with the PPUR people."

"Very astute, Kent. It was yesterday."

The first was long overdue and occurred at the insistence of the hospital. The Blue Cross people stressed its purpose was to "educate."

Some clarification of clerical issues was achieved at that one, but little else.

"Do you feel like sharing the gory details?"

"There are none. Actually, I thought things went rather well."

"Who is this, and what have you done with Dr. Czop?"

"No, really, Kent, it went okay. It's all still pretty absurd, but I'm not going to get anywhere trying to get them to realize it, so I'm just putting the energy into working through it and moving on."

"That's good. That's *very* good."

"And how are things with the U.S. Attorney's office?"

"Dead silence, and that's good, too."

"Okay."

"How's the home front, Doctor?"

"Better, thanks."

"And how is work?"

"I'm pretty much on target there."

"Good."

"How are you, Kent?"

"I'm in the middle of a huge case, and frankly it's got me pretty drained at the moment."

"Well, buck up."

It was early December, 2000.

"Really, Rich, don't you think that's enough lights?" Ellen asked.

"I just have one more strand. I thought I'd just go around that tree at the corner of the house one more time and that's it. I really am enjoying this."

Surgeons have performed operations in less illumination than what was radiating from the front of our house. Ellen had all the decorations up inside. As we stood out front on the sidewalk, Amanda came out to take a look.

"Yikes," she said. "I'm going back in before anyone recognizes me."

"Yeah, that's okay," I called after her.

She got to the porch and took a last look around and just shook her head.

"You two are *so* weird."

"Thanks," we answered. We had all the affirmation of normalcy that a ten-year-old could provide her parents. Ellen and I kissed and went back in, trying not to trip over any extension cords.

Christmas Day was beautiful. Everyone was home for the holidays: Kathleen from Africa, Meegan from Western Michigan U. with her boyfriend, Amy from Michigan State with her boyfriend. I remember sitting there smiling most of that day and thinking how lucky I was to just know people like this, let alone to have them be my family.

"This is exactly how I always wanted things to be," Ellen said to me when we finally fell into bed that night. "Thank you, Rich."

"I love this," I answered.

We were going to survive this. Actually, we were all going to better ourselves by going through the experience. That was my mindset as 2001 began. I had my job. I had worked hard to have it, and I would have to continue to do so to keep it. Only eleven more years, and I'd be able to retire.

Ellen tipped me off to a few books on anger management. I did not just read them; I outlined, studied, then re-read them. It made me sick to learn the potential negative impact of my behavior on my wife and daughters and I realized irreparable damage had already been done. I was doing all I could to not perpetuate the problem.

I stayed on the Paxil. Whether I was being treated for depression and/or PTSD did not matter. What mattered is that it made life easier for me and everyone around me. The only side effect I was aware of was delayed ejaculation, which took the only pleasurable human activity that has no calories and is not taxed, and turned it into work (nearly).

CHAPTER 14

On June 28, 2001, I had a meeting at the hospital's administrative office scheduled for 7:30 a.m. I hoped it would wrap up quickly. How long could it take to sign a new contract? It was Thursday, and today's and tomorrow's schedules were packed. I was already planning the rest of my morning. As soon as I got back to my office, I'd be calling my main cardiologist to get two people set up for urgent heart caths. He knew me well enough that it wouldn't take much talk or time to get these folks lined up, then I could still start my morning on time.

Kenneth Herron, the hospital CEO was at his desk and Bob Shaker, the man in charge of practice management, was in a chair opposite. They looked to be in good spirits.

"Good morning, Rich," Mr. Herron said.

That was different. In all the time I had known him, I didn't ever remember him calling me Rich. It was always Doctor Czop. I had finally arrived. I eased myself into the empty chair next to Bob.

"I'll cut straight to the quick, Doctor. I'm not renewing your contract, and under the circumstances I think it would be best that you not return to the office. We're going to make it for no cause, although we have cause, but I don't want to get into that. We're going to give you three months of severance pay, and we're going to waive the non-competition clause. Our preference would be that you resign, but if you choose not to, it'll just go down as a non-renewal."

There was silence.

"Unbelievable," I finally said.

Mr. Herron continued.

"You're struggling to reach the $320,000 minimum and from a physician of your experience, we're actually looking for more like $350,000-370,000 per year in charges. We don't think that would be feasible for you."

I thought for a moment.

"It would be difficult, but you've already made your decision, so it really isn't necessary to discuss feasibility."

"This is the most difficult part of my job, Doctor."

"I can imagine. I'm a little surprised, given the fact that all year long I heard nothing except that I was on track numbers-wise. I've done everything I could do to be there. I was optimistic about next year. I was hopeful that the PPUR business would be over in the near future and ultimately, I'm looking forward to being vindicated in the federal case."

I paused for a moment and just shook my head. The room was quiet. Then I continued.

"I was ready for this two years ago when the FBI came to the office. At that time, whatever your reasons, you hung in there with me. The system has put in a lot of extra time with my improvement plan, then in dealing with the PPUR. I'm walking away with skills in coding that I didn't possess two years ago. I'm grateful. I thought we had all weathered a bad storm together. Well, I appreciate what you did and, who knows, maybe this isn't all bad. I gave it my best shot. I've been pushing hard, and if this is what has to happen to get a little break, it's not all bad."

"Doctor, I appreciate your professionalism very much."

"Yeah, well, we all have our jobs to do. I'm proud of my work and glad for the opportunity. The sun will come up over all of us tomorrow. I'll have to talk with my attorney about whether resignation or non-renewal is the best route for me, given all the dynamics involved. I should be able to have an answer on that for you in the next hour or two. Does either course affect the severance pay issue?"

"No. Either way, you'll receive that and any other bonuses to which you're entitled. We'd just prefer it go down as a resignation, but otherwise it'll just be a non-renewal."

"Well, I'll get you that information."

"Good. Doctor, you have a devoted following of patients. It should be relatively easy for you to open an office. I can give you the names of some resources to help get you started with that. When you have a phone number and an address, let us know, and we'll put out that information to your patients and copy and send their records."

Going back into private practice while still facing a federal felony charge and being unable to directly bill the largest third party payer in the country just didn't sound like something that I wanted to run right out and do, especially after having just been fired, for all practical purposes, with zero notice.

"Actually, they're patients of Sparrow Health System, gentlemen, and since I'm no longer an employee, their care is your responsibility. I'm uncertain as to my future plans at this time. I hope you take as good care of these people as I have. It won't be easy, and I don't think they'll settle for anything less. Good luck."

I stood up, reached into my pants pocket, and struggled to remove something.

"This is for you two."

They suddenly looked tense. I took out a reflex hammer and set it on the desk.

"This belongs to the hospital."

"Now there's a first," Herron said as a smile and a look of relief crossed both of their faces.

"Again, Doctor, we appreciate how you're dealing with this," he continued.

"Yeah. Thanks. I understand, and I wish you success."

Everybody shook hands; I left.

Of all the emotions that I had experienced in that office, the one I walked out with was relief. It's a difficult job, but I was doing it. Forty hours a week of face-to-face patient contact was only part of the time involved in rendering good care. I was exhausted.

Once in the car, I called my wife.

"Would you like to go out for breakfast?"

"I can't; I'm cleaning the oven. Was your meeting cancelled?"

"No, we already had it."

"What happened?"

"I don't have a job anymore."

"Mr. Herron, this is Kent Haverman. Thanks for taking my call. I'm in my office with Dr. and Mrs. Czop. He's informed me of your meeting this morning and the unfortunate news. I need to know whether or not the Doctor is the subject of any internal investigation by the hospital?"

Ellen and I listened in silence until Kent spoke.

"Good. Now does anything involved in his dismissal constitute a National Data Bank entry?"

The response caused Kent to say "good" again. There's a national registry that keeps track of serious problems that involve doctors.

"I've advised him that he should not tender his resignation and that the matter simply be handled as a non-renewal. I'll draft a letter to that effect, and tomorrow, if the Doctor approves and signs it, I will fax it to you. If there are any problems, please call me."

Kent hung up the phone.

"What do we do, Kent?" I asked.

"Well, I don't think this will have a negative impact on your case. You've been a good boy as far as Sparrow Hospital is concerned. You've complied with everything they've asked of you. You've rendered good care. I do not think we need to do anything just yet. Take some time. Relax. The U.S. Attorney is not talking to you. They've arrested and dealt with everybody else in that sting operation. Let's just give him awhile longer to see if you are something he still wants to pursue. We have got some time here."

"Okay."

"Actually, Doctor, as far as your charges are concerned, losing your job is not all bad. This may sound cynical, but in essence, what Sparrow has just said is that you couldn't steal enough to meet minimal productivity criteria for employment there."

"Gee, Kent, I feel better already."

CHAPTER 15

I had been dealing with a vision problem that had been evolving for most of the past year. A scar-like membrane had formed in the back of my right eye, and it was causing the retina to pucker, in effect, creating a hole in the macula, the site of best visual acuity. Now seemed like a good time to get it fixed.

The surgery, a vitrectomy, involved peeling the membrane off the retina, after which a bubble of some kind of gas was injected into the eye to keep the retina from detaching. I needed to be face-down for at least ten days while the bubble was reabsorbed.

My first day back vertical and bubble-less, Meegan called and told Ellen and I to put on the television. It was September 11. Together we watched as the twin towers fell.

About a week later, I made a call.
"Hello, Kent Haverman."
"Hi, Kent."
"Well, Doctor Czop, how are you?"
"I'm doing pretty good. I think I have an idea that might be just short of brilliant."
"I'm all ears."
"I'm going to re-enlist in the Army."
"Ours?"
"Very funny. Just hear me out on this."
"Be assured that you have my undivided attention."
"I have no job, and given my current circumstances, it is unlikely I

will ever find a job."

"I do not think that is a given, but I will play along."

"Okay. For all practical purposes, we are at war or about to be. The military is going to need doctors."

"True."

"What would become of the case against me if I were to re-enlist?"

"Interesting."

"Yeah."

"Then the U.S. Attorney would have to decide if the public interest would be better served by chasing you around for a few more years or by allowing you to serve your country in a time of armed conflict. Doctor, I think we both know the answer to that."

"Bingo."

"Are you serious about this?"

"I've already talked to the recruiter. I would go in as major and get credit for my prior service. The money would not be what I was earning before, but right now that is zero, and we are not going to fly too long on that. It sounds like the solution to all of our problems at the moment. I could live cheap, and my family could stay where we are until we see how it is and then go from there."

"You know something, you might just be right. I see only one problem with the plan."

"What?"

"How do you feel about getting killed?"

"Most likely I would be stationed in the States, and they would send younger legs overseas. I'd fill a spot here that they would be vacating."

"Ah, I think you'd better get that in writing."

"I'll keep you posted, Kent."

"Doctor, as usual, it's been interesting, to say the least."

The Army encountered no legal impediment to my re-enlistment and sent me in for a physical. Not long after it, I got a call from the recruiter.

"Doctor Czop, it's Sergeant Dodd."

"How are you?" I asked.

"I'm okay, Sir, but you're not. The Army reviewed your physical and stamped resubmit in nine months on it."

"Do you know why?"

"No."

I contacted an old friend, Senator Levin, for help again.

A few weeks later, I learned that there was a mandatory one-year waiting period for entering the military after a vitrectomy, and that there are no exceptions.

The case reassumed its roadblock position in our lives. In nine months, we'd be in bankruptcy. I was afraid the prosecutor would think that I had tried to manipulate him with the idea of reentering the military and be pissed. There was no way to know that except to wait and see. Just beneath the surface, Ellen was terrified. She had gone to work in a friend's medical office. That helped. She kept busy, and there was income, but I had to find something, and soon.

Since the day that the FBI had walked into my life, I had wanted to sit down with a psychologist who had experience dealing with veterans who had been in combat. I had two reasons. First, I wanted to find someone who could verify and validate the total risk and threat that I perceived and experienced in the undercover investigator's second presentation. Second, if it came to a trial, I would need an expert witness who could testify to those facts. I turned to the Veteran's Administration.

Dr. Bill Buxton served in the infantry in Vietnam at the same time I did, came home when I did, and graduated from Wayne State with his bachelor's in psychology at the same time I did. It was almost scary. We had probably sat in some classes together. He went on and got his Ph.D. in clinical psychology. We had lived parallel lives through difficult times and had become successful, useful citizens and family men. The connection between us was immediate.

"Personally, I'm shocked and saddened by what you've told me. Professionally, I'd be happy to testify on your behalf in any setting."

It felt like the weight of the world was being lifted off my shoulders.

"I can see you on any basis that you think might be helpful. I think it would be a good idea. You're under a lot of stress."

"I'd like to do that."

"Are you on any medication at this time?"

"I'm taking 10 mg of Paxil every day."

"Good. Continue with that. Do you receive any disability from the VA?"

"I get something for the chest wound I had."

"Are you getting anything for post-traumatic stress disorder?"

"I have had trouble coming to grips with PTSD; I did not want to think of myself as being disabled by a psychological disorder. I mean, my best friend is quadriplegic because of Vietnam. Now *that's* disabled."

"Is he working?"

"Yeah, he is."

"Are you?"

I was silent for a moment.

"No."

He had made his point. He continued.

"Having PTSD is kind of like seeing the world with sunglasses on. You can see, but the view is different, and there are times when it would be better to take them off, but you can't."

"I guess I figured that if I did not accept it, it did not exist. I managed to go on."

"Your defense against it was to run hard and not look back, and that worked for a while. You should apply."

"I think I'll wait until I find a job. The resume is a little hard to sell these days: accused federal felon, can't directly bill the largest health insurance company in the country, lost last job for failure to meet minimum productivity standards. Now, we're going to throw in that I'm a little wigged-out from Vietnam. Oh yeah, and I'm a 54 years old. With that story, I am not likely to hear 'wow, you're just what we've been looking for.'"

He laughed.

"You have done well, and you will again. I will do anything I can to help you."

I was overwhelmed. My mind was racing, reprocessing years of my life. There was so much to think about and so much that I wanted to say. I settled on two words.

"Thanks, Bill."

"Welcome home, Doc."

As I walked out, the chill happened and my eyes filled. Thirty-two years later, I was still saying "Thanks, Bill" to a guy who was going to help me survive Vietnam. I began to see him on a regular basis.

In late November, 2001, Ellen made a suggestion.

"Why don't you go to Toronto for a few days, Rich? There will be no one bugging you, and you can get some serious writing done."

I interpreted that to mean, "You're in a bad place again. Do us a favor; get out of here for a bit before you ruin another Christmas."

In 1982, I had actually begun writing "The President and Some of My Other Friends" while riding with friends on a train to Toronto for a weekend getaway. I returned to that city several times in the course of completing it when I needed a distraction-free block of time. After the FBI walked into our lives, writing once again had seemed like a safe and effective way of dealing with the emotional aftermath.

"We don't have the money for that," I countered.

"We'll find it," Ellen answered in a tone that said this was not a topic for debate.

"Okay, how about this: the six hours each way is what I really need. I'll just stay in the station for the few hours between trains and not book a hotel."

"Deal."

After starting the Paxil, I stopped writing because, basically, I didn't give a shit about much of anything anymore. At the time, I welcomed that. I wanted to live and keep my family. The clinical term is anhedonia, or, a blunting of emotional responses. That, and delayed ejaculation, were side effects best tolerated. Now, writing something that might help other veterans better understand PTSD and accept help for it sounded therapeutic for all concerned. I needed to re-read what I had written pre-Paxil and decide whether it was worth going off the med to finish what I had started.

"Your citizenship, please," the customs officer asked at the Sarnia Station, the first stop over the border in Canada.

"United States."

"What's your destination in Canada?"

"Toronto."

"And what's the purpose of your visit?"

"Basically, I'm just taking the train ride to work on something I'm writing. I'm just turning around and taking the first train back."

"And what is it you're working on?"

I'd crossed this border a hundred times and never had anybody from customs talk to me this long. It was understandable post-9/11, but what did they think I was going to do - hijack the train and take it to Afghanistan?

"I'm writing a book."

"May I see it?"

"Okay."

I reached into my briefcase and pulled out fourteen file folders, each containing a chapter with its title on the end tab.

"Here it is."

"Would you fan through the pages for me?"

This was getting ridiculous. I did as he asked. As I fast-flipped through the first chapter, he stopped me.

"Hold it! Go back a few pages."

I did.

"There! What's that?"

Out of three hundred-some pages, he spots the one with United States Department of Justice written across the top.

"May I see that please?"

I handed it to him.

"What's this?"

"That's what the book is about. Those are charges that were brought against me. They were dismissed."

"Do you have the dismissal letter?"

"Not with me. I'm almost done with the book and am just basically reading and editing what I've written. I left that home with a bunch of other resource material that I don't need right now. I could call my wife and have it faxed here in five minutes."

"May I take this for a few minutes?"

"Sure."

He exited the car. About five minutes later, he returned with another customs agent.

"Sir, would you come with us please?"

They led me into the next car, which was empty as far as I could tell. The new guy spoke.

"I'm sorry, Sir, but you cannot enter Canada. Even though these charges may have been dismissed, you still have an active FBI number. You'll have to disembark here at Sarnia, and we'll take you by car back across the bridge to U.S. Customs in Port Huron. You'll have to sign a form there, then you can be on your way."

"Where to?"

"You can go wherever you want other than Canada."

"Unbelievable."

"We're sorry."

"It's okay. I know you guys are just doing your job. It's just been one thing after another with this case. It just doesn't stop. Oh, well, I got a few hours of work done from East Lansing to here. Just tell me one thing."

"If we can."

"This is mostly about 9/11, right? I mean, you guys aren't still pissed about the Wings winning the Stanley Cup a couple years ago, are you?"

They both laughed.

"No, we're over that. We'll bring the Cup back home again soon."

"Good luck. The Wings are looking tough."

"Good luck to you too, sir. You come back and see us when you get this all straightened out."

"Okay, thanks."

"Hi, Ellen."

"You can't be in Toronto already."

"I got as far as Sarnia and now I'm in a Holiday Inn in Port Huron. I had to use my credit card."

I explained what had happened.

"Unbelievable. Are you okay?"

"Me? Oh sure, I'm fine. Do you know where I could get some phony ID that says I'm an Arab, and I just want to come into your country to learn how to fly 737's except for landings and takeoffs? They don't seem to have problems getting around."

"I don't blame you. I'm bitter, too."

"Bitter? No, I'm not bitter. I'm just glad you had me take that enriched plutonium out of my briefcase before I left."

Ellen laughed. Then she added, "I guess that just leaves Mexico."

"Hello, Kent Haverman."

"Hi, Kent."

"Doctor, or should I say, Major Czop, how are you?"

"Not good, Kent. You can call me by my real first name,

Defendant. The Army thing fell through."

"I'm sorry. What was the deciding factor?"

"It wasn't the case, it was the eye surgery. There's a mandatory one-year waiting period before you can enter the Army after that type of surgery."

"From the way we're heading militarily, that may be a blessing in disguise."

"Yeah, maybe, but that's not why I called."

"What's up?"

"I have a couple things. First, do you remember back a ways when I said <u>The United States vs. Richard Czop</u> was not a fair fight, and they might better get Canada and Mexico on board?"

"How could I forget?"

"Well, they're down to Mexico."

I proceeded to tell him of the previous weekend's events.

"Unbelievable. That shouldn't have happened. There are no formal charges pending against you at this time. I'll look into this."

I realized that not having formal charges did not mean the case was over.

"Whatever. It's not like I'm going to go back there for a while, but someday I'd like to."

"Fax me the paper you got from customs. I'll get back with you on this."

"Okay. The other reason I called was I'd like to get something from Blue Cross about the PPUR. Am I still on that? I haven't worked in six months."

"I'll put in a call. There's never been a legitimate reason for you to be on PPUR, let alone to continue it under the circumstances. They've just been reviewing Sparrow Health System policy and procedure by shining the spotlight on you. Hopefully, they'll see that now, although I've told them that all along, and it hasn't mattered to them."

"Well, I've got to tell you, Kent, I've just about had it with all this bullshit. What more can they want from me? There's got to be something legally screwed up with all of this. I mean, they're not God."

"Close, very close. They're powerful, protected, and they were pissed at you, but it's time they get over it."

"Yeah. It is."

I stopped the Paxil; I had another chapter to write.

Kent talked to the head of Blue Cross/Blue Shield criminal investigation. Things sounded favorable. A third meeting with the PPUR people was proposed. It sounded like they were about ready to wrap up on it. After he told me about it, I summarized things.

"So, I have to go back down there and basically kiss the big blue ass one more time."

"Doctor, your command of the English language never ceases to amaze me. Basically, you're correct."

"I'm worried, Kent. I'm starting to feel desperate again. I'm thinking ass *kick*, not kiss. Is there any way you could go with me to the meeting? You have a nice way of keeping me from making matters worse. I need you to be close enough to choke me if necessary."

"Yeah, I think you're on the right track. Go ahead and set it up."

One of the PPUR ladies met us at the security desk in the nice building in Southfield. She had been at the first meeting, but not the second.

"Hello, Dr. Czop. We can head upstairs now."

"This is Kent Haverman, my attorney. I asked him to accompany me today."

"You didn't inform us that you'd be bringing your lawyer with you."

"I didn't know I had to."

"I'm sorry, but if you're going to have legal representation present, then we have to have one of our attorneys present, too. Without any notice, it won't be possible to arrange that for this meeting."

I turned to Kent.

"I'm sorry, Kent. I didn't think there'd be any problem with this."

"Yeah, you should have let them know. I assumed you would. I should have confirmed that."

"It's my fault. Should we reschedule this?" I asked the lady.

Before she could answer, Kent spoke.

"It's okay, Doctor, I can wait down here. If you need anything, you can call me."

"Thank you, Mr. Haverman," the lady said. "If that's acceptable to you, Doctor, we can go ahead and meet."

"Yeah, okay. Let's get this over with."

Not only was I without Kent, I was off Paxil. We went to a different room. It was a standard small conference room, but one entire wall had a mirror from mid-width to ceiling. There were two people I had never seen before seated at the table.

"Dr. Czop, this is Dr. Haggarty, one of our physician reviewers."

"Nice to meet you," we both said as he stood, and we shook hands.

"And this is Cynthia Barrett from the PPUR administrative staff."

We nodded across the table to each other and said something pleasant as we all took our seats. I faced the mirror so anyone I assumed was behind it could easily note my facial expression. Why else would a conference room have a mirror halfway up one wall?

"Doctor, how are you?" the lady in charge asked.

"Well, it's a little difficult at the moment. I believe you're aware that I didn't have my contract renewed at Sparrow. It was a little hard to meet their productivity standards while being forced to be inefficient and having my most frequent visits down coded. And it's a little tough when my old patients call and they're sick and I can't help them. But that's not what's really important, is it? Let's get to those coding problems."

There was that corporately correct silence, diverting of the eyes, and a little paper shuffling.

"Shall we begin?" one of the ladies said.

"By all means," I answered.

"Well, most of your submissions are being approved now. There's just one area that seems to be a recurring problem. Dr. Haggarty will address that. Dr Haggarty."

"These forms that you're using for well-baby and well-child exams, I don't think they meet criteria. I-"

"Wait. Let me guess, you think that they should be dictated, right?"

"Well, that would probably be better, yes."

"For who?"

"For us to approve payment for those visits."

"Those are Sparrow Health System forms. Everybody uses them. They're perfectly adequate for recording and documenting what was done."

"Well, it's not clear who's recording the data. Is it the nurse, the doctor, the patient, or the parents?"

"Yes, it is. They all have input."

"Well, that's confusing."

I ran my hand down my face from forehead to chin and tried to get a grip.

"Doc, what's your specialty?" I asked.

"Internal medicine."

"So you don't take care of infants, kids, or adolescents?"

"No."

"Don't you feel just a little bit unqualified to judge how well these forms address the situations they're used for?"

"Well, the criteria are readily understandable and-

"Okay. Right. I give up. I've tried to tell your predecessors the prohibitive cost of dictating and transcribing notes for routine things that readily lend themselves to forms. In family practice, these types of visits are a gift from God. The patient is *well*. We monitor growth and development, do an exam, give the immunizations, pass out some anticipatory guidance stuff, check off some boxes. Then we move on to a chronically ill person who's going to take more time than they're scheduled for, but it'll all work out because you can make up the time on a few well kid exams, unless we have to write all that out or dictate it."

I looked at him, then the rest of the people in the room, all looking down at the table in front of them, patiently waiting for the maniac to stop trying to explain the real world consequences of "the guidelines." It was pointless.

"Be assured that if I ever work again, the first thing I'll do is revise these forms or do whatever it is you want me to do. Okay? Will that do it for you people? No one can afford what you're requiring of me. I give up. You guys win. Tell your boss I was here, and I was non-compliant, uncooperative, belligerent, and whatever else you want to say. I don't care anymore. I'm done."

"Doctor, I don't think we'll be accomplishing anything useful today, so I suggest that we adjourn and reschedule at a later date," the lady in charge suggested.

"Really? I disagree. I think this has been most enlightening. We've got the essence of the problem with healthcare delivery right here in front of us. I don't think it can be any clearer as to why it's falling apart. That's useful. Insurance companies are at the controls of a 747 flying straight into the ground, and we're talking about the upholstery on the seats. Good luck."

"Well, Doctor, we'll transmit our information and be back in touch with you."

"Yeah, sure."

I didn't slow down as I walked past Kent, who was sitting in the lobby, and headed for the door. I just turned my head and said, "I've got to get out of here."

He caught up with me out front.

"Let me guess. It didn't go well."

"No," I answered without breaking stride.

We had driven about a mile before either of us spoke again.

"Do you want to talk about it?" Kent asked.

I proceeded to tell him what happened, and then I wrapped up.

"I'm sorry, Kent. But I've had it with this whole goddamn thing. Sometimes I find myself making plans to do some damage."

I paused.

"I just don't know how much more of this I can handle."

"It's okay, Doctor. You were entitled to what you did back there today. You've done everything everybody's asked, and it's still not over. We'll just let the dust from today settle a little, and then we'll see where we have to go next. But don't beat yourself over the head for today. You needed to say what you said, and frankly, they needed to hear it."

The next day I restarted the Paxil.

CHAPTER 16

It was February, 2002. For all practical purposes, I had given up. I hadn't worked for ten months, and I didn't care if I ever did again. Savings were nearly gone. A year earlier, I had signed up to go to Detroit Tiger Fantasy camp in Lakeland, Florida. One of my patients had been after me to go for several years and I kept putting him off, but since the last time, a forty-eight-year-old doctor buddy of mine had just died of complications of a stroke. At his wake, atop a pedestal next to his casket was a framed picture of him in his City Baseball League uniform with a bat on his shoulder. Pedro Rivera and I used to communicate well with a minimum of words. This time, I got his message without any.

When I told my two nephews about it, they signed up, too. At the time, I thought it would be a nice break in what was supposed to have been a busy year. After losing my job, I nearly cancelled the trip. Ellen wouldn't hear of it.

"No kid on earth ever needed to play for a week more than you do," she said when we had talked it over. "Go have fun with your nephews and just forget everything else."

Baseball was important in our family. My parents had been huge fans. After my Dad's brain cancer surgery, I went into the recovery room and watched as he started to wake up. Without opening his eyes, he slowly and precisely raised both hands to his bandaged head, thereby proving he still had good motor function. Then, with one question, I got all the confirmation of his cognitive abilities I needed.

"Dad, who are the Tigers playing tonight?"

He opened his eyes and looked at me like I was an idiot.

"Boston."

February 3, 2002 finally arrived. Walt, his younger brother Mike, and I sat at the gate in Detroit Metropolitan Airport waiting to board the campers' plane for Florida. I looked at my nephews. These guys always made me feel like someone special. Just to hang out with them for a week would be a great thing. We would be playing baseball together, the three of us, with players from the World Championship teams of 1968 and 1984.

The first morning, we had just finished breakfast, and we sat down in the hotel lobby waiting for the shuttle bus to Tiger Town. The man seated across from me reading the paper looked familiar. It was Willie Hernandez, winner of both the Cy Young and Most Valuable Player awards in 1984. His screwball simply could not be hit. I could see him on the mound with his hat like an upside-down teacup smashed over the world's largest Brillo pad. He had a short haircut now.

"Willie, I'm honored to meet you. My name's Rich. Thanks for what you did with the Tigers. Those were amazing moments for me and my family."

"Well, thank you, I appreciate that very much," he said with warmth and sincerity. We reached across the space between us and shook hands.

"These are my nephews, Walt and Mike."

"Nice to meet you, Willie," both said as they shook hands.

The three of us chatted, and he made us feel like we were long lost friends of his. Another guy walked up.

"Hi, you guys headed out to the ballpark on the shuttle?"

My mouth refused to form words; Walt had to take over.

"Yeah. I'm Walt Czop from Hartland. This is my brother, Mike, and this is my Uncle Rich."

"Al Kaline. It's nice to meet you all."

One by one he shook hands with us. I don't know how I looked, but it must have been a lot like how I felt.

"Is your uncle okay, Walt?" Al asked.

"Yeah, he'll be fine. He's a little blown away with all this."

"Well, I'll see you all out there."

"Yeah, okay, Al, we'll see you at the ballpark," Mike and Walt said.

The three of us just looked at each other. Finally, I was able to speak.

"Yeah, okay Al, as in Mr. Hall-of-Fame-On-The-First-Ballot, as in Mr. Batting-Title-In-His-Rookie-Season Kaline, we'll see you at the ballpark? Tell me this is really happening."

"It is, old-timer. Just take it easy," Mike reassured.

The clubhouse at Tiger Town with was huge. Rows of wire mesh cubicles with wooden benches across their fronts filled it. The floor was carpeted. The walls had large photos of past Tiger greats, and in the corner where we found our places was a large mural of the '68 championship team. People spoke in hushed tones. This was hallowed ground. On a bar in our spots, our home white and away gray uniforms and hats were hung. On the back of the jerseys were our last name and the numbers we had requested. Down the aisle came Ted Berger.

"Hey, you made it! What do you think?" he asked. "Isn't this something?"

"Unbelievable. Thanks, Ted, for turning us on to this. These are my nephews, Mike and Walt, also known as numbers "2" and "10," respectively."

"Nice to meet you guys."

"You, too, Ted," both said as they shook hands.

I stood at the plate in a Detroit Tiger uniform. At the side of the cage was Al Kaline, Mr. Tiger; on the mound was John Hiller, 1968's late inning closer and Cy Young Award winner who saved forty games that year. Both looked like they could still play. This had to be a dream.

"Ready?" Hiller called out.

"Yeah," I answered.

His first pitch was about two-thirds of the way to the plate when I swung and nearly fell down. Mike and Walt cracked up. Al spoke calmly from the side of the cage.

"Okay, Rich, you can wait a little longer on the next one and maybe not swing so hard. Ratso's not trying to strike you out, and I don't see any scouts around."

"Yeah, okay. Thanks."

"Ready?" Hiller called in.

"Ready."

I shut out everything and focused on the ball as he released it. I studied it, waited, swung; I just missed and didn't lose my balance.

"Better." Mr. Kaline said so.

"Here we go," Hiller said.

I locked out who was throwing and who was watching; I knew what to do. I connected and sent a liner out over the infield.

"That's it," was the word from the mound.

"Good stroke," came from the side of the cage.

I proceeded to bang out a few solid hits, interspersed with a few dribblers.

"Okay, Rich, nice work. Next batter."

"Thanks, Al, and thanks, John."

I grabbed my glove and trotted out to third base. The infield grass was like a putting green - the dirt smooth and free of stones. I felt like I should take my shoes off so as not to mess anything up. I had just taken batting practice with John Hiller and Al Kaline. In line to have the same experience shortly were my two nephews. Instead of being pinched to come back to reality, I tore my right hamstring going for an easy ground ball.

After breaking for lunch, our team assignments and game schedules for the week were posted. Ted had gotten us all on the same team; Dave Bergman and Mickey Lolich were our coaches. We put on our away uniforms and headed to the field for our first game. I had a six-inch ace bandage wrapped tightly around my right thigh.

"Okay, Doc. Keep your nose pointed directly at the ball. Have a plan in mind as to what you want to do. Make him throw you a strike, and take a nice swing at it."

"Got it, Dave."

"Strike one," the ump yelled.

"Doc," Coach Bergman called out from the dugout. "Why didn't you swing at that?"

"I never swing at the first pitch."

"That's what I thought. Don't lock yourself out of an opportunity. The first pitch might be the best one you'll see."

"Okay, thanks."

It was good advice, and it came from the man who once had what Sparky Anderson called "the greatest at bat in my life." The 1984 team had thirty-five wins and three losses at the time. They simply refused to lose. With the score tied 3-3 in the bottom of the tenth inning of a nationally televised game the night of June 4, 1984, Bergman went to a three ball/two strike count then proceeded to foul off seven straight pitches before belting a three-run, walk-off homer into the second deck in right to win the game. Thirteen pitch at-bats are rare; another one that ended in a walk off extra inning win had probably never happened before.

The next pitch was on its way. This one looked good. I hit it solid. I came out of the batter's box thinking I'll look for it when I get to second base. After three strides, I felt my left calf tear. When Gates Brown had advised us at the morning's orientation, "Start slow, and taper off," I had no idea how slow he meant. There was an amendment to the pinch runner rule which allowed for the guy who made the last out in the previous inning to run from home plate for a player who couldn't anymore. Apparently, I wasn't the first fool to come down here and have his "inner child" put in touch with his "outer grandfather." After the game Coach Bergman called us into a group.

"Gentlemen, I'm impressed. We had our ugly moments, but we were pretty strong on the fundamentals and got the job done. Walt and Mike, you guys looked like you could play for real, nice game. Doc, what can I say? At least all your parts are still attached. Way to hang in there. Tomorrow, we play two games, and it's going to be warm, so dress for it and drink lots of water. Does that about cover it, Mick?"

Lolich, the hero of the 1968 World Series, had been sitting on the bench with his eyes half closed. He was nursing a case of bronchitis. He looked up when Dave said his name. He got to his feet and surveyed the group for a moment, then drew a deep breath.

"Yup."

Then he sat back down.

The next day, we took a six-run lead into the last inning, but we came unglued and suffered our first loss. Bergman sat us down on the bench.

"Gentleman, this game is all about failure."

He let his words sink in before proceeding.

"You go to the plate, and if you get a hit just once in four tries, you're good. If you get a hit once in every three tries, you're in the Hall of Fame. That means that two or three out of four times that you try, you're going to fail, and when you do, you sit down and think about what went wrong and come up with what you might do different next time. You make a plan, pick up the bat, and step back up to the plate. There's no disgrace in failing, just in not trying again. You guys let yourselves get away from sound fundamentals out there today, and we let one get away from us. We can be a better team because of it if we refocus and give it another try tomorrow. Is that about how you see it, Mick?"

Lolich was doing better today. Yesterday, he talked me into putting him on an antibiotic for his bronchitis. He looked us over, rolled his lower lip over the top one, then spoke.

"Yup."

"Anything you want to add?" Dave asked.

Mick stood and put his hands on his hips.

"Nope."

Our team went 6-1, but we lost in the championship game. Now, it was time for the Fantasy Game - the campers against the pros. Each team would have an inning on the field, and each player would have one at bat. We were introduced one by one by the PA announcer, and we lined up down the third baseline, then the pros were introduced and lined up down the first base line. Then we all sang the National Anthem, which wasn't easy with the huge lump in my throat.

I stood in the batter's box.

"Doc, it's been good being down here with you this week."

Bill Freehan was catching.

"Thanks, Bill. I can't tell you what this has meant to me. Thanks for all your help."

Staring in from the mound with a look of absolute non-recognition was Mickey Lolich. I was at the plate between the pitcher and catcher from the 1968 World Series, one of the greatest in the long history of baseball. Lolich won a record three games and cracked a home run; the Tigers came back from being down three games to one. His first pitch was on its way.

"STEERRIIKE ONE!" the ump bellowed.

I had never seen a baseball do what Mickey's knuckleball just did. It seemed to be floating in slow motion when I swung at it, and suddenly, it was in Freehan's mitt. The second dropped like it had been shot; I missed it by at least a foot. I swear the third was on its way back to the mound at one point in its flight. There was almost enough time to swing again after my first miss. I had struck out on three pitches.

"Foul tip," Freehan called out as he threw the ball out of his glove onto the ground. "I wish I could have held on to it. You're still alive, Doc."

It was a gift. I stepped out of the box to re-orient. I looked out to the mound.

"I saved your life for this?" I yelled to the mound.

"Here you go, Doc," a laughing Lolich called to me.

This one was another gift: right down the middle with nothing on it. I caught it solid. As the ball climbed into the sky over right field, I took a few stumbling steps toward first. I had made good contact, but out there in his "office" was Mr. Kaline. Forget about it.

Then it was time to go.

"Dave, you have no idea how important this week has been for me. I can't thank you enough for all the time you spent with my nephews and me. I'm ready to go home and try again, and if it doesn't work, I'll try a new plan."

"Doc, I've been doing these camps for a lot of years now, and I can tell you for a fact I've never enjoyed one more. You, Walt, and Mike are special people. Keep in touch."

CHAPTER 17

Before I could walk without a limp, I was back to full-time work. In August, 2002, I called Kent.

"I haven't heard from you for a while. I don't know if that's good or bad. I need to check with you on a couple things. First off, I've been working at Haslett RediCare for three months, and they want me to sign a contract. They need to know my status with the case and PPUR."

"I was just about to call you. I have good news for you. The U. S. Attorney's office wants to wrap up your case. They've decided to offer you what's called prosecutorial diversion. It's a favorable resolution for you. I'd like you and Ellen to meet with me as soon as possible so I can more fully explain the process."

"Doctor, Ellen, good to see you again."

"It's been a while, Kent. I was actually starting to miss you," I said.

It was doubtful that either of us had slept. We wanted to believe that something good was about to happen, but we didn't want to get our hopes up too high.

"From what Rich told me, Kent, you have good news," Ellen added.

"Yes, Ma'am, finally; it's called prosecutorial diversion."

He passed out copies of the prosecutor's letter that explained things in legal terms, and then proceeded to translate.

"Basically, what it means is that the government is not going to seek a conviction against you. Instead, they'll set some conditions that you'll have to meet, which will involve some sort of an admission on your part that you did something wrong, and then they'll probably put you on probation for some period of time. They may or may not require you to perform some amount of community service. You first have to meet with a court officer to determine if you are to be accepted into this arrangement."

I sat there in silence. There had to be a trip wire somewhere in the vicinity.

"Assuming he's accepted, what happens then?" Ellen asked.

"Then the matter is concluded without prosecution. It's finished, and there's no record of a crime being committed. In essence, folks, what this means is you've won."

Ellen heaved a deep sigh, and her eyes instantly moistened. The end was in sight, the end of three years of hell. Her relief was obvious.

"What about holding out for a trial?" I asked.

Kent and Ellen simultaneously hung their heads for a moment before he replied for both of them. All the fight had long since been drained out of Ellen.

"Doctor, you don't want a trial. We've done the math on that before. You can't count on how a jury is going to feel about a matter like this. You're a doctor. To them, you're rich, you manipulated the system, and you got caught. That's what the average person on a jury is going to see and hear, despite whatever else you tell them about the motivation for your actions. Trust me. Talk to Randy and any of your many attorney friends and see what they tell you. I understand how you feel. It's been an unfortunate and difficult sequence of events, but the end is in sight now, and legally, the outcome is as good as we could have hoped for."

I just shook my head, looked down, took a deep breath, and slowly exhaled.

"Kent, I appreciate all your hard work on this, don't get me wrong, but please forgive me if I don't feel like throwing any confetti. This whole goddamn thing is a crime committed against me and my family. We're the victims here, not the government, and now after they make me jump through a few last hoops, all this never happened?"

Kent was silent. I continued.

"I wish it was that way for us. Amanda was nine when this all started; she'll be fourteen before it ends, if it does. She's lived almost half her life not knowing if her world is going to blow apart at any given moment. I have no idea what she thinks or understands about any of this. We've gotten help for her, but she's locked up tight, and she keeps it all inside. That's who I worry about the most. The rest of us have a fighting chance of recovering."

It was quiet for a moment, and then Kent spoke.

"Doctor, it's been a long, hard ordeal. I'm convinced that the worst is over for all of you."

I heaved another deep sigh; there was no sense saying more of what I had been saying for three years.

"Okay. What's next?" I said.

"Read the letter and talk things over, and get back with me with a decision in the next few days."

"Okay."

"Kent, thank you so much for everything," Ellen said as we rose to leave.

"Me, too, Kent. Oh, hey, before I forget, what about the PPUR thing?"

"You're not still on that are you?"

Prior to the meeting with a Pretrial Services Officer, a great deal of personal and financial data needed to be acquired, copied, assembled, and forwarded. Ellen did it all. All I had to do with the assistance of Kent was write down my confession. It read: "I was employed by Sparrow Health System as a salaried physician. An undercover officer, posing as a patient, requested time off work to play golf. I approved the time off by stating the patient had a back injury. He did not have a back injury."

On October 1, 2002, the meeting took place in the Federal Building in Grand Rapids, Michigan. After dealing with the basic formalities and then reading my confession, the court officer asked me why I did it. Neither she nor I

173

took our eyes off each other while I told her everything I had been waiting to say for three years. When I stopped talking, she continued to look at me in silence before turning her face toward Kent.

"And this is what this case is about?"

"Yes, Ma'am," Kent replied.

The disbelief on her face and in the tone of her voice was obvious despite her effort to mask it. She looked down at her desk, made a few notations on her paper, and then looked up.

"Doctor, please have a seat in the waiting area and send your wife in."

I walked out to Ellen.

"Your turn."

About fifteen minutes later, I was asked to come back in the office. No matter what might ultimately become of this encounter, we had had our moment to see a face on the prosecution side and tell our story for the first time. We both had tears in our eyes.

"Doctor, your and your wife's responses to my questions were identical. I don't hear that every day. I'm going to recommend that you be accepted for diversion. You and your wife have been through some difficult times. Hopefully, this matter can be concluded in a fashion acceptable to all concerned. I'll expedite my report, and you will be notified through Mr. Haverman. I've enjoyed meeting with all of you and I want you to know that Mr. Haverman has done a fine job representing you."

"Thank you," Kent answered.

"We know. Thanks again, Kent," Ellen offered.

"Ditto from me, Kent, and, Ma'am, we thank you for listening."

It was a good day and it got even better when we got home. In the mailbox was an envelope from the Veterans Administration. After going to work at Redicare, I made the claim Bill Buxton had recommended. It was approved, and disability for PTSD was awarded.

At Christmas in 2002 we were all together, with the exception of Kathleen, who had signed on with American Refugee Committee to work another year in Guinea, Africa after the Peace Corps. We were alive and well. In a way, the coming year would be harder than the previous three, but at least we knew what we were facing now, and getting through it seemed doable. On Christmas morning we opened presents, laughed together, and took pictures that Ellen later sent to Kathleen. As Meegan handed me a tiny little present, she made a short speech.

"Dad, I know that sometimes in the past you didn't think I was listening to you, but I always was. The other day I heard you say for the next year you're going to have to kiss every ass in authority in your world. I know that's not going to be easy for you, but this may help."

I couldn't imagine what it might be. I opened the package and held up the contents: three tubes of flavored Chapstick. Everybody cracked up.

"Thanks, Meegs."

Later, I taped two of the tubes together to get both lips with a single swipe in emergency situations.

I signed the final version of the diversion agreement on December 31, 2002. On January 9, 2003, I paid the Clerk of the United States District Court, Western District of Michigan Lansing Division $131 in restitution for the payments made to Sparrow Health System by the undercover investigator on his two visits. I would have to do three-hundred hours of community service, and I would be on probation for one year.

"Hey, man, show me how the hell you do that so fast."

"Naw, it's a gift. You've got to be born with it; it can't be taught."

I sealed the tape around the napkin that I had just tightly wrapped around the plastic fork, knife, and spoon, and tossed it into the box with the rest of them. With up to 200 people a meal and two meals every Saturday and Sunday, Advent House went through these little packets pretty fast. He held up his, and the knife slid out of the bottom onto the table.

"This is bullshit. Come on, man. Show me how you do it."

I stopped working and looked around slowly to the right, then the left. Then I looked at him and spoke in a hushed tone.

"Okay, but you got to promise you'll adhere to the code."

"What code is that?"

"You cannot tell anybody where you learned it, and you got to agree to teach somebody else."

"You serious?"

"Take it or leave it, man. You want to fumble-fuck your way through life, or you want to wrap your shit tight?"

He cracked up.

"What's your name?"

"Rich."

"Rich, I'm James. It's nice to meet you."

"You, too; here, watch this."

I showed him where to set the utensils and all the moves needed for a nice snug wrap.

"Damn, that's good."

After a couple minutes, he was batting them out like a pro.

"I knew as soon as I saw you, James, you had what it takes to do this. Nice work."

We both laughed.

"You a volunteer, Rich?"

"No, I'm court ordered community service."

"For real?"

"Yeah."

"DUI?"

"No, it was a federal thing."

"Get out of here."

I laughed.

"No, really."

"What did you do? Do you mind me asking?"

"No, I don't mind. I'm a doctor, and I gave an undercover

investigator a week off work."

"That's bullshit, right?"

"Yeah, it is, but it also happens to be true."

He just looked at me.

"You mean I'm sitting here at a soup kitchen rolling up plastic shit with a fucking doctor?"

"You got it."

He started laughing. Then I had to.

"How many hours do you got to do?" he asked.

"Three hundred."

"Three hundred!" he roared. "I stole a car, and I got one hundred."

At this point, we were both laughing hard. After he was able to get it together, he asked me more.

"Didn't you have a damn lawyer?"

"Yeah, I still do, and he's a good one."

"What'd that cost you?"

"Twenty-five grand to start."

James paused for a second, then broke out in a laugh that he couldn't stop. Everything that had been so devastating for so long suddenly sounded as hilarious to me as it did to him. Soon, we were both laughing so hard that people were looking at us, and tears came to our eyes. He got himself together enough to be able to talk.

"I paid mine 400 bucks, and I had to sell my car to get the money!"

"Well, cheer up. I had to sell my damn house."

I thought I might have to resuscitate James in the next few minutes, and I was laughing almost as hard as he was.

"Stop, Doc, you're killing me."

We both recovered for a second.

"James, until now, I couldn't even think about this without getting either sick or totally pissed off. Thank you."

"Doc, I've got to get up and take a walk. That shit is unbelievable.

I'll hook up with you later."

"Yeah, okay, man. Then I'll show you how to mop the floor."

"Okay, gang, it's eleven o'clock. Lights out. Let's hit it. I'll get you up at six, and breakfast will be 6:30. It will be damn good."

"Thanks, man, good night."

Half of the ten temporary residents, six men and four women, had already gone to bed. The rest headed to their bunks. Loaves and Fishes Ministry is a homeless shelter in a residential neighborhood in Lansing.

"Hey, man, you seen a pair of jeans around here?"

"Yeah, I'm finishing up that last load of laundry, and they're in it. They'll be sitting right here on this table for you in the morning."

"Thanks, Rich."

"No problem. Good night."

After the laundry was done, I went to the kitchen and took some bacon, sausage, and shredded cheddar cheese out of the freezer for breakfast. Then I went to the small bedroom/office reserved for the overnight staff person and laid down. It was 12:30AM when I set the alarm for 5:30 and shut the light. I never slept well there; I was always worried that I was going to sleep through the alarm, resulting in ten people not getting fed.

I got maybe a few hours in and was up five minutes before the alarm. I threw on some clothes, washed up, and headed to the kitchen. Three dozen eggs, two pounds of bacon, a pack of sausage links, grits, toast, and occasionally pancakes. I quickly got it down to a science. I was poetry in motion. At six, I'd run around and get everybody up. At 6:30, all courses were ready to serve. People's eyes would bug out of their heads.

"Say when on the eggs," I said as they held up a plate in the opening between the kitchen and the dining room.

"That's plenty."

"Bacon?"

"Sure thing."

"Toast?"

"Thank you."

"The grits are the best you'll ever have made by a white guy. If you find a lump, turn it in to Carol, Don's assistant, and she'll give you a quarter."

As we sat around the table that had been donated by the governor's mansion, people talked about where they were headed that day. Some had low paying temporary jobs. Some had to go to government agencies for assistance of varying kinds. The day staff opened many doors for these people, most of who had not caught a lucky break in years. If it was someone's birthday, I would call it in to a local radio show. A few residents even won lunches at nice local restaurants. Everyone had to be out by 8 a.m., and they could come back at 6 p.m. for dinner, then bed down again. Two weeks was the maximum stay. As they left the dining room, they would call to me in the kitchen.

"That was fantastic, man. Thanks."

"Glad you enjoyed it."

"Hey," another called out, "you were right about them grits. They were perfect. You sure you're white?"

"I must be. I got a vertical leap of four inches, and I can't dance worth a shit."

He laughed. "Have a good one, man."

"You do the same."

I cleared the table, washed and put away the dishes, jumped in the shower, then headed to Redicare just in time for my eleven-and-a-half hour shift. I did this once or twice a week. I wanted to complete community service as quickly as possible. I needed the nightmare to be over.

On August 14, 2003, having paid Blue Cross, completed my 300 hours of community service and stayed out of trouble, the United States Attorney's Office for the Western District of Michigan granted termination of the Diversion Agreement. The case was finally closed. I continued to volunteer at Loaves and Fishes most of the next year. They had helped me, I liked what I was doing, and I regretted that it took a legal action to make me serve my community in this way.

The government was done, but Blue Cross was not.

"I'm disappointed with the position Blue Cross has taken on your status with PPUR, Doctor."

Kent had been working on this as the diversion program was going on. When it was terminated, we both believed PPUR would end, too. I thought he was calling to tell me that.

"The Blue's criminal investigation department is giving you two options: another six months of PPUR, after which time it would be stopped if submissions are satisfactory, or end it now, and be subject to an audit in nine to twelve months, after which if submissions are satisfactory, the PPUR will end."

I couldn't bring myself to respond at first.

"Doctor?"

"Yeah, Kent?"

"It's not what I wanted to hear either."

"Kent, these people just used the FBI and the Department of Justice to screw up my life for three and a half years, and now this guy is going to cost me another job."

"I don't think that will happen. I know your boss. He thinks you walk on water. I think he'll do whatever he can to keep you there."

Redicare had neither the financial nor the manpower resources to deal with PPUR for six months. The option of ending it now, then having the facility be audited in nine to twelve months was even worse. It wouldn't take much of an investigation to turn up a few charts with coding errors at this or any other facility in America, including their own Blue Care

Network, after which the Blues would legally own you. On discussion with the owner of Redicare, we chose the continue PPUR for six more months option.

After many claims were either "down coded," reducing the reimbursement, or outright denied, cash flow plummeted. Unlike Sparrow, Barry Leffler was willing to challenge the rejections. I had to review each case and type a detailed explanation referencing the E and M coding criteria that justified the billing level claimed. In addition, I voluntarily took a 50 percent pay cut until such time as the appeals would result in the appropriate reimbursement. All this took time and energy above and beyond my eleven-and-a-half-hour work day, but it had to be done because all our livelihoods depended on it.

It took many phone calls, most of which were never returned, and several trips to meet with the PPUR people, but our appeals were successful and the rejection rate approached zero as the six months of PPUR neared its end. There were still twelve cases that we referred to as "the dirty dozen" that we maintained were coded correctly for which payment should have been forthcoming. Blue Cross felt otherwise. Barry and I refused to accept their position. He arranged what would prove to be our last meeting, this time with the chief physician overseeing the review process, a Dr. Dennison, whom I had never met.

Across the table from Barry and me sat doctors Dennison and Haggerty. Director Dennison's opening statement summed it all up for me.

"Let me begin by saying that it's not our function at PPUR to be educational."

Eleven of the dirty dozen were approved with minimal discussion. The care rendered was medically appropriate; the claimed level of service was justified and well documented. The last of the twelve was, too but Dennison was clearly frustrated. We had already won the game; it didn't need to be a no hitter.

We drove out of the parking lot, never looking back. We talked in the car on the way home.

"Boss, I can't thank you enough for what you've done for me and my family. All I was hoping for when I called was a few shifts to help pay bills. You didn't have to put up with the PPUR, but you did. You're a special person in my life."

Barry teared up; I did, too. He struggled for a moment with what he wanted to say next.

"I hate to see people getting kicked around."

After a little while, he continued.

"You've helped me just as much. As you know, I've had my problems. With the business going well again, I've had time to put my life back together. I got to mend some fences with my dad before he died. I've had more time with my son than I did in all the time he was growing up. The marriage has been rocky, but we're working on it. I just think we got sent each other's way for a reason. I really believe that. Nothing happens without a reason. I'm glad I know you, and I feel blessed to call you my friend."

"I feel the same."

The case was closed. I became the only physician to be removed from PPUR and still be able to directly bill Blue Cross administered insurance programs. I guess we were all supposed to live happily ever after, but the United States vs. Richard Czop had been a dirty war, and no one wins those.

"Why don't you go meet Wayne Tanigawa and the boys in Las Vegas for Superbowl like old times?" Ellen had asked as 2004 began.

Wayne was a friend from the dorm at MSU who lived in Honolulu. We hung out a lot when I was at Schoffield Barracks, and I got to know a bunch of his buddies. After a gap of 17 years, we started hooking up in Vegas on Superbowl weekend. I didn't go while the case was going on; I would have had to get permission from my parole officer, and I didn't think it would look good. What happens in Vegas may stay in Vegas, but what took place in the privacy of my office between what I thought was a patient and I became a federal case.

"Why don't you go with me?"

"No, that's a stag thing, and you know I don't like gambling."

"Yeah, but I could just hang out with them game day, and the rest of the time could be ours."

"I don't feel up to it, but you should go. You've earned it."

"So have you."

"Maybe later on you could take me somewhere, but go ahead and be with your friends."

Allegiant Airlines flew direct from Lansing to Las Vegas with discount fares in those days. We were boarding for the 7 AM departure.

"Excuse me, Miss, I've got the window seat."

"No problem," the woman on the aisle answered as she shifted to make room for me to get by.

All I generally need from the person in the seat next to me on a plane is that they fit well in the chair; a pleasant disposition is nice but not a necessity. I got settled, the plane took off, and I took out some continuing medical education materials to study. Thirty seconds later, I put them away; there was nothing in them I would need to know for a few days in Vegas.

"Who do you like in the Superbowl," I asked the woman next to me. I really didn't expect her to know anything about it; I was just making conversation.

"It's going to be a good one, but Carolina's never been there, and Tom Brady not only has, he was the MVP. Besides, he's a Wolverine. My name's Cathie. You a football fan, too?"

I just stared in disbelief. She was attractive, too.

"Ah, my name's Rich, and yeah I like football, but I been kind of busy this past season and don't know much about Carolina."

"Well they're good, don't get me wrong, but put your money on

Brady, and you won't be sorry."

That's how the conversation started, and it never stopped until we got off the plane. She was from Grand Rapids, and this was the first time she had travelled in a while, too. In the back of the plane were seventeen of her friends who talked her into making the trip. A year-and-a-half earlier, her fifty-two year old husband of twenty-one years had gone to the spa, finished his workout, and was sitting by the pool reading the paper when he dropped over dead. Her friends figured it was time for her to get back to living.

At first, she was careful in talking about herself, but as we shared some history she felt more comfortable. She said she worked for the State of Michigan, but she was reluctant, almost embarrassed, to tell me what she actually did. It turned out she, her friends, and her late husband were all Corrections Officers working in the men's prisons in nearby Ionia. A year after her husband died, she retired as a captain after twenty-six years on the job. The noisy crowd in the back of the plane was her people, who were still working "inside."

"Why wouldn't you just come out and say what you did for a living?"

"Well, some people see Corrections as a low-end job, and besides that, we like to make sure who we're talking to," she answered.

"Low-end job, are you kidding me? I can't imagine a more psychologically complex working environment. You folks work with the most dangerous people on the planet, and if I'm not mistaken, you don't carry weapons."

"That's true; the prisoners could get them and do some real damage."

"And you did that for twenty-six years, rising through the ranks the whole time?"

"Yes, I did."

"That's incredible; you had to master the subtleties and nuances of human behavior to recognize danger and deal effectively with it, or you would not be sitting here. I know what that's like because I was in Vietnam.

At least they gave me a rifle. Most people would not even attempt what you considered 'just your job' for twenty-six years. You should be proud."

"Well, thank you. I appreciate that."

It was not long before I shared with her my experience with the undercover investigator and its consequences. That opened the flood gate. She was one of the first women to work inside a men's prison in Michigan. She started in women's facilities but switched because she found the women were too sneaky and unpredictable. She had slugged it out with the Department of Corrections over a legal case involving PTSD and won. She had an experience with the IRS that resulted in her having to sell off her riding stable and forty horses when she was in her early twenties. She was obviously a people person, strong willed, duty-bound, not one to tolerate being beaten down, and most clearly of all, a survivor. I felt like I was sitting next to the female version of myself, except for the fact that she was a rabid University of Michigan football fan. Nobody is perfect. She loved cooking, grew a wide variety of peppers, and prepared and sold eighteen varieties of salsas. Near the end of the flight, she handed me her business card.

"Rich, if you ever want to buy peppers or salsa, you just call the Jalapeno Mama."

"Okay, thanks. I'm not much into that kind of stuff, but you never know. Hey, I have really enjoyed talking with you. I hope you and your friends have good luck in Vegas."

"Same here, and good luck to you, too."

When I got back home, Ellen picked me up at the airport. I spotted Cathie in the baggage claim area. I asked her how Vegas went, introduced her to Ellen, and wished her a good life. That was it. I was happily married; I didn't know my wife wasn't.

Over the next couple of months, it became painfully obvious that things were not right between Ellen and me. I think she made her decision when things were at their worst between us. She kept it all inside while we battled against the three common enemies and our individual demons.

After "our victory," it was time.

"I cannot live like this anymore. You take too many chances that put the family at risk. We have nothing in the way of a retirement or pension plan, and we are running out of years to start building that. I cannot fight anymore, with you or anybody else you have a problem with. I have to think of Amy, Amanda, and myself from here on."

We separated near the end of 2004. The divorce ending our 19-year marriage was final in November, 2006.

PART THREE

CHAPTER 18

I first started seeing Dr. Buxton in 2002, and I had been seeing him at regular intervals since. He was driving from his office in Grand Rapids to the Lansing Veteran Center to see several clients, but by January, 2005, it was just me. When I found that out, I told him that I could drive to Grand Rapids to see him so he wouldn't have to spread himself so thin. After several trips, I remembered the Jalapeno Mama lived there. I looked in my desk drawer for the business card she gave me; I always keep those. It had been a year since we had met on that flight to Las Vegas. At this point, Ellen and I had been separated for seven months, and she was in the process of filing for the divorce. I found the Jalapena Mama's card.

"I don't know if you remember me; this is Rich. We met on the plane going to Vegas."

She had to orient for a moment.

"Oh yeah; for crying out loud, how are you?"

"I'm okay. I have some business in Grand Rapids this morning, and I was just wondering if there was any chance I could take you out for breakfast afterward?"

We met at a restaurant near her home on April 26, 2005. It was nice; nothing more, nothing less. She was in the middle of organizing the third annual memorial golf outing for her deceased husband, with proceeds going to the Mel Trotter Ministry for the homeless in Grand Rapids. She gave me a flyer and hoped I would sign up a team.

I could not put one together, but I signed myself up for the event, and she placed me with three of her friends. I saw her before and after the round. I was impressed with the fact that she was honoring her deceased spouse in this way. She organized this event, brought their friends together for a day of fun and commemoration, and gave the proceeds to a local charity. It was obvious that this was a special person, and that the corrections employees shared a special camaraderie that grew out of watching each other's backs in a dangerous environment over time. I liked that.

We started seeing each other. After a few months, we were spending a lot of time together. I was living in an apartment in Williamston and working at least three shifts a week at Haslett Redicare. On weekends, I was welcome to stay at Cathie's place. Her basement was finished, and there was a couch/bed and a bathroom down there.

"That's yours. You are married, and this as close as we get to each other until your divorce is final. Take it or leave it."

Late that summer, Kathleen was home for a visit, and she invited me to go to a movie and out for drink after. She wanted to talk to me. While I was waiting for her in front of the theater where she had once sold popcorn, Meegan called me.

"How are you, Dad?"

"I'm fine, Meegs, how about you?"

"I'm good. Has Kathleen talked to you yet?"

"I'm waiting outside the movie we're meeting up to see. Has she talked to me about what?"

"Well, we're concerned about you. You seem so happy lately. What's going on?"

"I've started seeing a lady."

"Oh, thank goodness! We thought you had either gone gay or were running a meth lab."

Right then, Kathleen came walking up. I told her about the

conversation I had just had with her sister. She hugged me.

"Thanks, Dad. What a relief."

A few days later, she was headed back to her job.

Kathleen had spent three years in Guinea, Africa, two in the Peace Corp, and then one with American Refugee Committee, teaching women's health (mainly HIV prevention and treatment) to battered female refugees coming out of war-torn Sierra Leone. Because of the case, I had been unable to visit her. Currently, she was teaching English as second language at The International School of Phnom Penh, Cambodia, and she wanted me to come and see her. Cathie and I talked with her regularly on Skype.

I wanted to make the trip, but there was only one problem. Our schedules afforded just one opportunity, and that was during the week of Cambodia's annual Water Festival, during which a million people descend on already overcrowded Phnom Penh.

"Dad, we can't stay in the city, and I have seen enough of the temples of Angkor Wat. Would you consider going back to Vietnam? It's a short boat trip away, and I could put together a super package for us at great rates."

"No."

"It might be good for you to do that. Would you at least think about it?"

"Okay. There, I just thought about it. No."

"I really want you to come see me, and you'll never have a better opportunity to travel to this part of the world and have me as your guide. I'll plan the whole thing. Please."

Cathie was all for it. It was October, 2005, and we had been seeing a lot of each other since April. She knew I was carrying a train-load of baggage into our relationship, and she felt dumping some of it back in Vietnam might be a good thing. Arguing with either of them individually was challenging; taking on the team was pointless.

My pride in my daughter overrode any other feelings I might have had about being back in Southeast Asia. The International School of Phnom Penh was where the children of the aristocracy of Cambodia and of the highly placed governmental and non-governmental workers from other countries attended elementary and high school. Kathleen showed me around the facility and introduced me to her fellow faculty members, after which she and I toured the city.

Like all of Southeast Asia, this country's history was fraught with near continuous war. North Vietnam and Cambodia were allies in the 60's then enemies in the 70's. In the last half of that decade, Cambodia came under the rule of Pol Pot and the Khmer Rouge, whose "agrarian reform programs" relocated most of the population of Phnom Penh to the countryside, where from one to three million people were either systematically worked and starved to death or executed.

Around 1998, Cambodia began a movement to become a weapons-free society. Over the next five years, a cache of 125,000 leftover military weapons, mostly AK-47's in civilian hands, was created by exchanging them for tools like plows and sewing machines. Some of the military hardware was turned over to The Peace Art Project in 2003, and artists and their students used them to create amazing works of art. We visited the museum where they were displayed. Weapons were forged into new shapes and relationships creating flowers, birds, animals, people, and furniture. The pieces alternately whispered and screamed their messages about the horrors of war and the power of the human spirit to overcome them and heal. The next day a colleague of Kathleen's from Wales, Rob Jones, and I played golf at the Country Club of Cambodia, the site of a former a killing field.

The boat that took us to Chou Doc, Vietnam, was basically a fast water-bus that carried about twenty people. There were several checkpoints along the way where we had to get off, show our passports, and talk to Cambodian or Vietnamese military and government personnel. I was uncomfortable with all of them because of the old "who was the enemy" issues. It did not matter that this was thirty-six years later. My daughter knew her way around this part of the world and kept me informed as to how to conduct myself. Things went smoothly on the four-hour trip.

We arrived at our first two night's accommodation, five-star Victoria Hotel. I took a nap while Kathleen went off to orient herself. When she came back, she had hooked up with a local business owner who would give us an all-day guided tour starting after breakfast tomorrow. We had dinner and called it an early night.

We were at the breakfast buffet the next morning. I was starved so I went for the closest item; Kathleen did some recon work on the total layout.

"Dad, I think I found something you might want to see."

In the past, I had told the family about this amazing fruit that grew wild in Vietnam and how every time we spotted it, the tracks would come to sudden stop, guys would go chop off a few and pass them around. They looked like a cross between a big pink tulip and an artichoke on the outside, but when cut open, the inside was white with tiny black seeds and had the consistency of a citrus. It was sweet, wet, and refreshing, especially when we were hot and dehydrated. Through the years after I came home, I described it to people, and even the Vietnamese did not know what I was talking about.

I got up and followed Kathleen to another section of the buffet. She stopped and pointed to the table.

"Is that it?"

There it was behind a sign that said "Dragon Fruit." I was just reconnected with a long-lost friend from the war by my daughter who did not exist at the time. Tears kept running down my cheek all through breakfast.

Mr. Phon and a friend of his, each on his own motorbike, picked us up in front of the hotel after breakfast. We introduced ourselves and chatted for a bit. The tour almost ended before it began.

"Your daughter has told me that you were a soldier here during the American War," Mr. Phon innocently stated.

Obviously, the glorious conquerors had educated him with their spin on history.

"Ah, no. Actually, I was here during the Vietnam War, the one where North Vietnam invaded South Vietnam, and the United States tried to help prevent the takeover. Unfortunately, the South never matched the North's passion for the fight, and they lost."

He got a puzzled look on his face. It seemed for a moment like he couldn't get it, didn't want to, or was afraid to be caught listening to anti-government propaganda.

"I am sorry. I meant no offense," he responded.

I had no bitch with the South Vietnamese; they lost more than I did in the war. Rather than ruin both of our days, I let him change the topic. After a few minutes, we were ready to go. We straddled the seats behind them, put our arms around their waists, and the day's touring began. He was a successful local business man, had a family, and proved to be an excellent resource for the grassroots history of the area. He and Kathleen had decided our itinerary the day before. Instead of places tourists would visit, he took us mostly to the homes or shops of people he knew, and we were welcomed as if we were family. Despite generations of war, they looked happy and sounded hopeful. I bought their goods and ate their homemade foods. This was the area where I had been a soldier carrying a rifle. Today, I was a father with his daughter shooting photos of other parents trying to raise children and live in peace.

We ranged all over the city and countryside. At one point, we stopped to visit a beautiful Buddhist temple. While inside, some sort of service or ceremony started, and I did my best to chant, kneel, bend, and bow like everyone around me. At the end, we all took a burning stick of incense and placed it in a trough filled with sand. The crowd was made up mostly of older women, and the chanting involved repeating a short phrase over and over. We were very near the place where I had listened to a woman cry out "help me, I dying," all night. She could have been any one of these women if she had lived, praying to Buddha for good fortune or maybe even for peace.

After the service, I went and sat down on a bench off by myself.

The women filed out and were all a-buzz as they talked to Mr. Phon and kept smiling and nodding in my direction. He and a couple of them came over and he told me they were impressed and grateful for my attempt to participate in their ceremony and show my respect for their beliefs. I looked at their beautiful, smiling faces and heard their voices. They were honoring me. Kathleen knew about the woman we probably killed, and she saw that I was struggling with this moment. After the ladies left, she came over and put her arm on my shoulder, and I lost it.

We took our hosts out for dinner, and it was dark before we finished. Darkness here, now, was like a curtain gently coming down to end a great day, not the cloak that terror and death had hid themselves behind during the war.

We checked out of the Victoria the next morning and took a minibus to Saigon, nowadays known as Ho Chi Minh City. "Uncle Ho" was the leader of North Vietnam during the war years. Saigon was the capitol of South Vietnam. It was difficult enough to accept that he had won, but renaming Saigon for him was like a kick in the nuts. Going there was like simultaneously dishonoring our dead and kissing his ass. I did not want to do either. The road was rough and narrow, and the longest time without the horn blowing was no more than twenty seconds. It was difficult to think much about the past when life looked like it would be over in the next one hundred yards ahead of the bus. We stayed in a nice hotel in the center of the city, and that evening after dinner, we walked through parks and stood in front of Reunification Palace, where the North Vietnamese tanks rolled to a stop on April 30, 1975, ending the war. The next day, Kathleen booked air and hotel for two nights at a resort on beautiful Phu Quoc Island. It was off the coast of Cambodia but claimed and controlled by the Socialist Republic of Vietnam. For two days, we lounged on the beach under the palm trees, floated in the pool, ate the local cuisine, and talked.

"Dad, I need to say some things to you. You may not want to hear them."

I was pretty sure I knew what was on her mind.

"Say what you need to, Kack."

"This is not easy for me. I have stuff from my early childhood that I'm getting help to work through. You were not easy to be around sometimes, and sometimes you were down right mean."

I didn't say anything as I thought with shame back to the days she was talking about.

"Kathleen, you were basically a battered kid. Is that it?"

"Yes, Dad," she responded. There was both relief and surprise on her face and in the tone of her voice. She waited to see if I would say more.

"I was brutal. A spank is one thing, but I did it too hard, too often, and worst of all, when I was angry. I was not what you deserved as a father, and I am sorry for that. I hoped someday I would be able to sit down with you and tell you this. I should have done it long ago."

Kathleen hung her head, and tears came down her cheeks as she responded.

"Yeah, it wasn't easy for me; it still isn't. Thanks for saying that. I had a lot less trouble with the divorce than with this."

"I'm sorry, Kathleen, for all of it. So much of what I did was wrong in those years. I'm proud of you for being able to talk to me about it, and I am proud of the person you are."

"This is going to help me, Dad. I know things were not easy for you back then. I'm glad we can talk and help each other now."

We hugged for a long time. That this moment of healing and peace between father and daughter was happening here gave it profoundly greater significance. I think it was all linked together. People overcome events through love. Without love, there is no hope, and without hope, there is no reason to go on. We were both moving on, together.

We flew back to what I now accepted as Ho Chi Min City. We went to a classy spa near the hotel. Kathleen was into that sort of thing. I was not, but I tagged along. Women went to one part of the facility and men to another. I was led to an area where I showered, took a dip in a scented hot tub, stepped out, and put on a warmed thick robe, and had a cup of tea. Next, it was time for my massage. A beautiful Vietnamese girl directed me to a cushioned table where I laid down, and she discreetly replaced my robe with a towel over my private parts. She started working; I liked it.

Near the end of the session, she was working on my hands. When she got to my right index finger, I had a bad moment. Long ago, my brain and every muscle in my body were trained to kill the enemies of my country. I had been taught the necessary skills, and I carried weapons whose use I had mastered, but it was my right index finger that ultimately translated that knowledge and that firepower into action. With a squeeze on a trigger or a pull on a grenade pin, I crossed a line to a place there was no coming back from. There was no amount of massaging by this beautiful young girl that could change the fact that before she was born, I had come here to kill her people. I had tears in my eyes when I asked her to stop.

"Do I hurt you?" she asked.

"No, you didn't," I answered, struck by the irony of her question.

I made a feeble attempt to explain what I was feeling, but she did not speak much English, and I did not really have words for it anyway.

Shortly after, I met up with Kathleen.

"You have to admit, that was great wasn't it?" she said to me.

I told her what happened.

"I'm sorry, Dad - I shouldn't have made you do this trip," she said.

"No, this was a good thing. I have learned a lot. I have come to understand that nothing can change the past. Today and tomorrow are all that really matter. Being here with you has given me the opportunity to experience the amazing person you are. What happened to me long ago should not have been a problem for you or anybody else, but I let it be, and I apologize to you for that. I understand things better now."

We put our arms around each other held each other for a long time.

"Dad, I am so proud to be your daughter. I love you so much."

CHAPTER 19

Cathie had a way of making the major conflicts I faced less complicated and easier to resolve. I was reluctant to get married again because I did not want to risk another divorce. We discussed my feelings, sort of.

"Don't worry - I don't believe in divorce. I would shoot you first."

"Well thanks for working that through with me."

"Sure. You know what your problem is, Mr. Psychological Bullshit? You think too much."

"You know what, Ms. Ready-fire-aim, you talk too much."

"Maybe if you listened better I wouldn't have to."

In April of 2007, we were asked to stand up for friends (corrections people, of course) who were going to Las Vegas to get married. We accepted, and the four of us flew out together. On arrival, we rented a car and took them to the Clark County Marriage Bureau to get their license. Since they are good for a year, we got one, too. You never know, and we were right there.

The day before their ceremony, we got good news. I missed working in urgent care and had been meeting with a doc about a job in a Spectrum Health System facility in Grand Rapids. He called, offered me the position, and I accepted. Cathie and I were ecstatic. After breakfast with our friends, we went to Paiute Resort, a golf facility hidden in the desert and mountains north of Las Vegas. A patient of mine tipped me off about it ten years earlier, and it had become nearly sacred to me. Amidst the beauty and serenity of the setting, I believe I have felt the presence of the Great Spirit, and divine intervention is the only explanation for some of the shots I have made there. Cathie felt the same way about it. Halfway through the round, we talked seriously about our situation.

We were living together, I was about to leave working in an occupational medicine office in Grand Rapids for something I enjoyed more, and we were about to have a free-standing condominium unit built. We had gone back and forth on the details of when, where, and how we might get married. Then the Great Spirit sent a message. We both pared the next hole - big medicine because we're not that good. After the round, we picked up a bottle of champagne and went to the Little White Wedding Chapel. If they had a spot it would be the final sign.

"You guys got any openings for tonight?"

"As long as you don't want the Elvis Drive Through ceremony we do."

We booked a simple package that included twelve photos, some flowers, and a simple silver band for me. Cathie had what had come to be known over time as the APR (all-purpose ring: promise, engagement, and now wedding). When we got back to the hotel, we knocked on our friends' door.

"Hey, you guys got any plans for the evening?"

"Not really; what do you guys want to do?"

"The limo is picking the four of us up at 7 p.m. We're getting married."

The ceremony was performed by Reverend Belinda and could not have been more impressive to us if we were in St. Patrick's Cathedral. Our friends stood up for us, and we would return the favor the next day.

We thought the Great-Seat-Assigner-in-the-Sky was done for the day after Paiute and the wedding place having a spot for us, but later that night on a quarter video poker machine at the bar in the Imperial Palace, Cathie got a Royal Flush for a thousand dollars, in hearts no less.

When we got home, I immediately went to work on the credentialing process for the new job. I assembled all the necessary documents, filed out the forms, and hand delivered them to the Medical

Staff Office to assure a successful and expeditious outcome. I was completely honest and up front about everything involved with the case and the resultant ten month gap in practice. I was assured everything was in order for a decision at the next meeting of the committee that oversees the process.

It wasn't. They wanted more information. When I provided that, the next month they wanted something else, and so it went for the next ten months. Nothing I, Kent, nor the FBI provided seemed to reassure them enough to allow me to be approved. I thought I had seen, heard, and worked through every personal, societal, and professional consequence of PTSD imaginable, but I was wrong. After the case and the second divorce, I put the hundreds of pages of related documents away and did my best to move on. Being forced to exhume and restudy them meant reliving the associated events, which were as painful and upsetting as they had always been. Rather than allow that to put the same pressure on this marriage, I withdrew my application.

"Sweetheart, if want more challenging work, why don't you try the prison system? They're always looking for doctors," Cathie offered.

I cleared the last of the five locked and guarded gates and walked down the hall in the Health Services Unit like I had for the past two years.

"Goddamn this piece o' shit;" I heard from inside our office.

"Morning, Mikey," I said when I walked in.

Mike Gibbs had been a physician's assistant in the Michigan prisons for thirty-eight years.

"Oh, hi, Doc. How are you?"

"I'm good. You all right?"

"Yeah, fine. Coffee's done."

"Thanks."

I poured a cup as Mike hit a few keys on his computer keyboard and then pounded his fist on the desk.

"How in the hell do they expect us to get anything done with these worthless-"

"You want a refill, Mikey?"

"Sure."

I filled his Marine Corps mug.

"Thanks, Doc."

I sat at my desk and turned on my computer. As it was booting up, I looked over at him, staring at his screen with his head tilted back so he could look through the bottom of his bifocals. On the side of his face toward me, he has a long, irregular scar. There's a similar one on the other side of his neck. His left forearm is missing a lot of muscle mass and has several long scars.

He and his best friend joined the Marines on the buddy plan and went to Vietnam together. They were on the DMZ when they came under attack. Mike was shot five times in an eight hour battle but still managed to grab his wounded buddy with one hand and pull him over his head back down into their foxhole. Both survived.

Seventeen operations and two years of rehabilitation later, he became one of the country's first-ever PA's. As difficult as this place can get at times, Mike and I have seen worse and that helped.

"What have we got today?" I asked him.

"Well, I have got to break the news to a guy with gender identity disorder that he does not meet the criteria for the department to provide him with a bra," he answered.

"You're kidding."

"Nope, and you have to work in a guy with a black eye."

"What happened to him?"

"The usual: he tripped, and a helpful guy nearby tried to break his fall with his knuckles."

Ted, the level two gate officer, poked his head in the office.

"Your first one is here, Mike," he announced.

"Bite me," Mike responded without looking up from his screen.

"Fuck you," Ted answered.

"Now, children, let's be nice, shall we?" I said without looking up from my screen.

We all laughed.

"I'll meet up with you for lunch, Mike. We have prime rib enchiladas today."

"Great, see you later."

Cathie started making lunch for both of us after I told her about some of the glorified road kill he would fix himself.

At 2:30 p.m., Mike headed for the door, where he stood in silence and watched me shuffle the paperwork that always covered my desk. I looked up at him. His gaze went from the clock to his cleared desk and then back to me.

"I know, I know. I've just got a few more things that I have got to get done."

Anne the nurse poked her head in the door.

"A guy just collapsed in Unit Six," she announced.

Guys "collapse" in here all the time. It's usually the new young ones faking seizures or faints to get something they want or to get out of following an order. It's less common in the older guys who have made the adjustment to prison life.

"I'll go, Doc," Mike volunteered.

"No, I need a break. I got it," I answered.

"Are you sure?"

"Yeah. Get out of here."

"Okay, thanks. See you tomorrow."

I grabbed my stethoscope and headed out, walking at a brisk pace.

"Who was it?" I asked.

"Sylvester Johnson," Anne answered.

I broke into a run and quickly covered the one-hundred yards to where he was. When I arrived, prisoners were milling around as officers did CPR on Johnson on the floor next to his bunk.

"What did you guys see?" I asked his bunkies.

"He just groaned, rolled off his bunk onto the floor. We couldn't wake him up, so we called the officers."

"Ambulance is on the way, Doc," the officers advised.

He did not respond when I called his name, he was not breathing, and he had no pulse. He was dead. The AED arrived, was applied, and showed ventricular fibrillation.

"Shock indicated," the machine appropriately advised.

"I'm clear, you're clear, everybody's clear," the officer confirmed before delivering the shock.

Johnson's body jolted upward in response. There was no change in his status.

"What do we do, Doc?"

"Resume CPR."

It was hopeless, but at least the spectators would recognize that we gave it a college try.

The machine advised another shock; it was delivered. I felt for a pulse.

"Resume CPR, Doc?"

"No, wait a second; he's got a radial pulse."

He took in a gasp of air. I shook him and called his name, but he made no response. I put a cuff on his arm and took his blood pressure. It was low but adequate to perfuse vital organs. The pulse disappeared and the monitor showed the rhythm had deteriorated back to fibrillation. Another shock was delivered and restored an effective beat but with frequent extra beats from the ventricles, a bad sign. He was taking some labored respirations but remained unconscious. Meanwhile we started an IV and the ambulance personnel arrived. There was a chance he would leave the facility alive but probably die on the way to the hospital in Grand Rapids. At this point, I ran back down to Health Services to get some records to send along with the ambulance. Johnson was in his sixties and had a complex medical history. I kept second charts on prisoners like him to assure quick access to vital data in urgent situations.

Two years earlier, he suffered a stroke secondary to a critically low heart rate, and a pacemaker was inserted. A cardiac catheterization identified a severe cardiomyopathy of unknown cause and for which there was no treatment other than transplantation. Twelve other medical diagnoses in his master problem list contraindicated that. There was no full-time doctor in the facility at that time; he survived because of the work of PA Gibbs.

There was another detail in his history that came to Mike's and my attention. On his coat, Johnson had sown the insignia of the 25th Infantry Division. Mike and I had both asked him about it and he proudly told us about having served in Vietnam. The details of where he was and what he did readily confirmed he was the real deal, not just another idiot with a bull shit story about having been a war hero.

The sally port was just behind Health Services, and I ran over and gave the second chart to the ambulance people. Johnson's heart was beating and he was breathing, but he remained unconscious and unresponsive to verbal or painful stimuli. After the mandatory search inside, outside, and underneath the ambulance, it was cleared and left the facility.

I returned to my desk to go back to work trying to prevent half a dozen or so other prisoners from becoming the next Johnson. When I had nothing left in the tank, I called Cathie to tell her I was heading home.

"You do remember we're going to Bonefish Grill for dinner tonight, don't you?"

"Of course," I answered, but she knew I didn't.

"Well, be careful driving home okay? I love you."

"I will. I love you, too. Bye."

"Oh, wait, pick up the mail on your way in. I love you."

"I will, and I still love you, too. Bye."

"Bye."

She says "I love you" a lot, and I have bought in, too. We have both said goodbyes that were never followed by another hello. You never know when it can happen again.

As I reached for the door handle at the control center, I was struck with the realization that the medic had just run across a hundred yards of enemy territory to reach the side of a downed infantryman who was given enough treatment to allow him to reach definitive care alive. The only thing missing was the chopper.

"You haven't heard a word I've said since we got here, have you?"

"I'm sorry, what?"

"Are you going to tell me about it or do you want me to leave you alone?"

I told her what happened. First, she had to tell me all the rules I violated in dealing with the situation. That's how things usually go. In her world, rules were to be followed to the letter. In mine, there was a time when all rules were suspended and later many got in the way of doing what needed to be done. After we each took a deep breath and a sip of our drinks, we were partners again, for a moment.

"I need to go to the hospital and see him," I told her.

"You need to *what*? That's just not done. You did your job, and now the hospital will take care of him. They wouldn't even tell you he's there."

This required two sips and two deep breaths each.

"Somebody's going to have to make the decision to take him off life support before he costs the state a million dollars."

I had a fighting chance with that line of reasoning, so I pushed it.

"He's got a complicated past history, and I was there for today's events. Who better to help assure the right decisions get made."

Cathie and I knew where each other was coming from: she knew I was going to go one way or another, and I knew when she settled down she would find a way to enable it to happen.

"There's no one by that name in the hospital," the lady at the desk informed me.

"Try the ER. He probably died there, or they may still be working on him," I answered.

She went back to her computer.

"No, he is not in the ER either."

"He's got to be here somewhere. He's a prisoner where I'm the doctor. He had a cardiac arrest, and we resuscitated him."

"I'm sorry, sir, but I see nothing about him."

I looked at Cathie; she had that Mona Lisa smile that I often elicited from administrative personnel at the prison.

"Rich, do you have your prison ID on you?" she asked.

"Yes."

"Ma'am, would you call and ask someone from security to come down here."

"Certainly," the lady answered.

A few minutes later, a man in a hospital blazer came down the hall. Cathie took care of the introductions and told him what I wanted to do.

"Here's his ID, and here's the number for the control center at the prison. Ask for the shift commander, and tell him where we are and what my husband feels he needs to do."

He disappeared for a few minutes, and when he came back, he handed me my ID.

"If you come with me, I'll take you up to cardiac intensive care. That's where he is."

Cathie and he exchanged Mona Lisa's; many security officers are former corrections people. By the time we reached the floor, my wife and the security guy were buddies with half-a-dozen acquaintances in common.

"Cathie, you'll need to wait in this area."

"I understand," she answered and took a seat.

"Doctor, he's this way."

We walked past several rooms where ventilators hissed, alarms beeped, and monitors displayed vital data in various colors in continuous fashion.

"He's in the next room. Come out when you're done."

Braced for the worst, I walked in. There were two officers I knew from the prison seated at the far side of the bed in which Johnson sat bolt upright, fully alert, with a keep-open IV in one arm.

"Sylvester, I can't believe this."

"Doc, do you know what happened to me? How did I get here?"

"Yeah, you died."

"No, really, Doc, what happened."

"You died. You groaned, rolled off your bunk onto the floor, and your bunkies could not wake you up. Officers worked on you and brought you back."

"Really? Were you there, Doc?"

"I stopped by for a little while, yeah."

"Praise God," he said with his face raised upward.

"Amen."

"Can I go back now, Doc?"

"You better hang out here for a day or two so they can do some tests and try to prevent this from happening again."

"Okay."

It was quiet for a moment; then he spoke.

"So the medic saved another grunt. Do you think this might be why we survived the Nam, Doc?"

"It just might be, Sylvester. What are the odds of us having been there, and winding up in a prison in Michigan with you on the ground and me kneeling next to you forty years later?"

With his medical history, they were probably better than his chances of being resuscitated by only CPR and an AED after a cardiac arrest and surviving without apparent neurologic or cardiac deficits after being down as long as he was.

"Thanks, Doc. Welcome home."

"Welcome home, Sylvestor. I'll see you when you get back."

We shook hands, and I was half way to the door.

"Hey, Doc," he called out.

I turned back around.

"I was doin' all day, you know, a life bit."

"Yeah, serving a life sentence, I know, so what."

"Well, if I was dead, doesn't that mean I-"

"No, it doesn't."

But it sure confirmed his intact cognitive function, I thought to myself.

I found my way to where Cathie and the security guy were sitting. By now, he was on her list for salsa and any extra U of M football game tickets we might someday have.

"How was he?" they asked.

I told them.

The next day, I brought Mike up to speed on what happened. Johnson was one of his crowning achievements as a PA. As I relayed the details, Mike listened intently. He did not say anything for a while, but I could tell where he was and what he was thinking by the look in his eyes, the thousand yard stare. After about fifteen seconds, he was back to the present. In a subdued voice, he said all he would say about this topic.

"Is he going to make it?"

"Yeah, Mikey, they're going to check him out and give him an implantable defibrillator. It will help for a while."

"Good."

Medical parole is not an option in first degree murder cases, but I sent in the paperwork for consideration of one anyway. His health problems were many, the cost for his care would be high, his life expectancy was short, and he was not strong enough to be dangerous to anybody. Then I looked into his case.

He volunteered for the draft and served as an infantryman in Vietnam in 1969. He was awarded the Combat Infantry Badge, the Army Commendation Medal, and he was honorably discharged. He came home to his wife, daughter, and son, and a country torn apart by opposition to the war and racial unrest. He graduated from Michigan Barber's School in Detroit, apprenticed for two years, got his certification, and went to work in a shop across the state.

All the while, he experienced full-blown Post Traumatic Stress Disorder: flashbacks, nightmares, anger, isolation, and fear. His Pre-sentence Investigation Report says his wife suggested psychological counseling to him, and quotes his mother, who stated "Sylvester has not been right since he returned from the service." He sought help but could not afford what little was available. An extramarital relationship led to a divorce in 1977. He stayed with the girlfriend for a while afterward. When he ended that relationship, she was angry and vindictive.

Meanwhile, another female acquaintance of Johnson's told him that a man he knew had tried to rape her. He confronted that man outside a South Haven grocery store and beat him up. Two weeks after that fight, Johnson's ex-girlfriend, still angry over their breakup, found Johnson at his sister-in-law's house. She said she wanted to talk to him, and he invited her in. She said she wanted to talk to him outside, so they walked to her car.

She and the man Johnson had beaten up had become a couple, and when Johnson opened the car door, he was lying on the seat with a rifle and opened fire. Johnson was hit in the left arm and chest, a bullet ricocheted wounding the ex-girlfriend, and another bullet went into the house and struck his seventeen-year-old niece in the heart. She died instantly.

The shooter went to prison. After he recovered, Johnson killed the woman with two blasts from a shotgun. Police arrested him without incident twenty-seven minutes later at his half-brother's house.

Psychologists finally diagnosed his PTSD in prison, and he received help from both the VA and the Department of Corrections for it. He participated in counseling for violent offenders and successfully completed programs in anger and stress management. He served as the prison barber. In an environment of constant danger, he learned to better process threat and to control his responses to it.

He could not tell his story, but I could. As a fellow combat veteran, and now as his doctor, I felt I owed it to him. I sent this information to the governor and because of President Obama's expressed interest in combat veterans in general and PTSD in particular, I sent a copy to him, too. I concluded with: "I believe he deserves the chance to re-experience freedom for whatever little time he may have left."

I never received a response from anyone, and Johnson was transferred to another facility.

Mike was better able to keep things in perspective, and he did his best to help me do that, but I was finding it more and more difficult to render care in the only way I knew how. The end came by mutual agreement. The Department of Corrections, Prison Health Services, and I had reached the limits our ability to cope with each other. I was making myself sick trying. On June 27, 2013, my regional manager, who stood by me and tried to help me from the day I started, came out to see me.

"Rich, I think you need to seriously consider getting out before you drop dead. You are a good doctor, but these institutions are bigger than both of us and they won't change to accommodate you. You've told me you are in good enough financial shape to retire; I think you should."

"I know. I agree."

"Why don't you finish out the week? I'll waive the two week notification requirement. Would that be acceptable to you?"

I thought about it before responding.

"If it is all the same to you, why don't I just clear my desk today and call it a career. I don't think anybody's best interest would be served by me having to see patients and tell them I'm leaving or act like I'm not and do business as usual."

"I think that would be best, actually," he responded.

"Yeah, let's go with that, then. Thanks for everything."

"You're a good man, Doc. I've enjoyed working with you. Please keep in touch."

I found a box, put my personal property in it, thanked and said goodbye to the facility's medical staff. What I thought was a grab for the lowest rung on the ladder of healthcare proved to be the site of some of my best and most gratifying work as a physician. Letting go would put me in a free fall; I was not sure what not working would mean for me. I did know I would need help. I drove directly from the prison to the VA, and the psychologist worked me right in. He listened attentively and then gave me good advice, as always.

"Finish writing your story."

When I look at our flag, especially while the national anthem is being played or sung, I see an armored personnel carrier driving fast across a dry rice paddy. On the 50-caliber machine gun sits a hippy-looking guy with a big mustache. The front of his jungle hat is turned up and the back turned down as he leans into the wind, the setting sun on his face. There are six other guys with M-16's sitting on top of the track. Taffy, the 4th platoon's black and white dog, stands facing forward with front paws on some gear, ears straight back in the wind, tail wagging. Tied onto the top of the track's long, flexible radio antenna is a small American Flag and underneath it is a smaller yellow one with three horizontal red lines. It was South Vietnam's flag. That country did not make it. We did. I did.

EPILOGUE

The transition from law-abiding citizen to combat soldier and back again is not as automatic and seamless as we would like to believe. The United States Marines Corps teaches that there is no such thing as an ex-Marine. Once a Marine, always a Marine. Though meant to acknowledge the lifelong commitment to honor and duty of members of the Corps, I believe the model is applicable in a psychological sense for combat veterans in general. Acceptance of that fundamental fact may help us better understand and calculate the ultimate "cost" of war and better serve those who have served.

Post-Traumatic Stress Disorder should be a diagnosis reserved for people with prolonged disabling psychological dysfunction after experiencing unexpected horrible events in the course of their otherwise normal lives. In war, horrible events are the norm, and an acknowledged consequence of the choice to serve. Using the same diagnosis to explain two fundamentally different conditions does not work. It stigmatizes a good soldier as having a disorder instead of being changed in ways they might not understand or even recognize. It understates both the magnitude and mechanism of the condition by equating it with stress, a benign, self-limited universal experience. An inaccurate diagnosis invites misdirected treatment plans.

How war ultimately impacts an individual is a product of a complex interaction of who they were before, what they experienced, and the subsequent availability of support systems. Family, friends, and faith may be adequate. In the isolation created by the absence of those, some turn to alcohol, drugs, sex, or antisocial behavior to deal with their emotional pain and psychological distress. The legal problems that may result can create a vicious, downward spiral with suicide as the last and worst option.

Some of the analogies offered to explain PTSD have helped me gain some acceptance of the condition, but thinking of myself as a "war-altered person" has served me better. The concept or term is a product of how I perceive certain situations because of having been in war, and what I subsequently learned about human beings as a physician. Maybe it can help someone else.

Neurologic activities such as movement, thought, memory, speech, and sight take place in specific areas of the brain like rooms in a house. How our sensory experiences are converted to biochemical data that can be stored is not yet understood, but the room where the storage takes place is well documented. It has a closet for the absolute worst memories of our lives, but the door has no lock. There are several ways the door can open. It can be accessed at will, but there is nothing good or necessary for function kept there, and you can close it again. When the brain needs to store new tragedies in that space, it has to open the door, and previously stored contents can start falling out. Sometimes, because the closet is overfilled, or its contents are so toxic and volatile, the door may blow open on its own.

In the last two scenarios, you need help to push it back closed before the past experiences can disrupt your ability to function effectively in your current circumstances. How much help and from whom will vary from person to person. Having insight into what is happening is an important first step. Accepting assistance needs to be recognized as a sign of strength, not weakness.

ACKNOWLEDGEMENTS

I am here because of the love and support of my family, friends, and patients who have stood by me through the best and worst moments of my life. In addition to those in the book, I would like to thank some very important people.

My niece, Lori Surge, is a brilliant beacon of femininity and joy in a family dominated by males.

Jim Hile was the first non-family member to hear about the case, and first on the scene with support and Chinese food. He was a sounding board for this story through its evolution from an angry diary to a possibly useful book. He led me to Bill Jack, attorney and author, who led me to Pierre Camy at Schuler Books, and the rest is history.

I had black hair and an Afro when Duane Stoolmaker started cutting my hair and listening to me talk in 1974; he still does both. Yogesh and Barbara Saxena, Bruce Johnson, Ernie Phillips, Frank (deceased) and Dora Garrison, and Stu and Sue Berry were there in the darkest days of 1999 and beyond.

Elvin Roy Culp and I were buddies during the last days in Vietnam and the first days in Hawaii. Forty six years later we reconnected in person. If I could live with a Wolverine for ten years, I should be able to tolerate one Buckeye in my life.

Special thanks to Mike Garrett who could have edited the first manuscript with a machete instead of a pen. His contribution to this book was the literary equivalent of what Dave Bergman's coaching was to my life.

Sarah Nicholas and Bill Andersen put the finishing touches on the editing, and provided encouragement.

Finally, Lorenzo (retired from corrections) and Dee (retired internist) Brown, who taught me that saying "okay, Sweetheart" works better than "what the hell are you thinking."

ADDENDUM – January 2026

After Prison Health Services and I parted ways, I had three goals: 1. Renew all my licenses and certification with the American Board of Family Medicine. I did that. 2. Credential with a locum tenens place and continue practicing medicine. 3. Finish writing PTSD AND ME.

I hadn't planned on getting diagnosed with prostate cancer and having surgery, temporary setback. Thank you, Agent Orange.

I went with Weatherby Healthcare and I was going to be placed at Community Hershey in Kokomo, Indiana. I was excited about it because I had started college in pre-med at St. Joe's in Rensselaer, Indiana in 1965. All I had to do was get an Indiana Medical License, "a mere formality." I did the paperwork, but because of having undergone prosecutorial diversion for the United States vs Richard Czop, I would have to appear in person before the Board of Medicine in Indianapolis.

I had to reschedule my first meeting because my brother, Walt, four years older than me and my only sib, was diagnosed with acute myelogenous leukemia. I spent 3 days at his bedside at University of Michigan hospital. He got seven days from diagnosis to death. My time with him was a gift to both of us.

The meeting in Indianapolis did finally occur. I expected a confidential encounter with 4 or 5 people. Instead, I was in a room with about 80 people, mostly docs who had lost their licenses for good reasons. I prepared a four-page dissertation to explain what I did and why. The ten or so board members paid little attention and even asked when I would be done. When I finished, they said: "okay you're not going to get an Indiana license, and you have two options. Either withdraw your request or have a National Data Bank entry saying you sought licensure in another state and were refused." I withdrew my application.

I found myself unable to resume working as a doctor, so I went to the VA seeking 100% disability for unemployability (I was already at 80% for a variety of conditions). I had a hearing and they awarded me 100%, but all for PTSD, which was better because I could still work and get the disability payments, unlike for unemployability (if I ever found work).

At that point, I only had to finish the book. By this time, PTSD was no longer a personal problem, it was a societal issue. I did what I could to make the story, which was never just mine, available to other veterans and their families. I was never able to seriously market the book because doing that kept me in a very dark place, and there were times when I was about done trying. Still, the book found its way to some people who said it helped them or a relative, and that was enough for me.

The event that proved life changing for me and the PTSD, was connecting with a high school classmate who had a basketball team in Birmingham Alabama. We hooked up in 2014 after not seeing each other for 50 years. I've been playing for Code Blue since. He and my buddy, Tom, ran cross country together for Detroit Catholic Central High School. Tom died November 24, 2024, 56 years after being rendered quadriplegic when his track was blown up in Vietnam in 1968. He got his Masters from Western Michigan University and counseled veterans. A few years ago, Cathie and I called and wished him Happy Birthday. I asked how he was doing. He answered, "not good." I asked what was wrong. He responded, "my van's in the shop." That summarized his life for me. He was the strongest man I have ever known. He was my best man in my first marriage in 1972.

With Code Blue consistently qualifying for the National Senior Games every two years, I always have a reason to stay in shape and look forward, instead of backward. We just finished 4th out of 16 (again) in the Des Moines Iowa games in July. We were beaten by the same three teams that did it in Pittsburgh in 2023. I worked my ass off to "shoot the lights out and not let us lose a game in Des Moines." At our practice the day before tournament play began, it looked like I was ready to do it. In our first real game, I took a charge from an elephant and wrecked my R shoulder. Cathie was shooting a video of the game. As people tried to help me get up off the floor, you could just hear the love in her voice as she called out, "Get up little white guy."

Now, it's back to the drawing board for 2027 in Tulsa Oklahoma. We'll be playing in the 80-84 bracket. I'll be 80 and a "rookie," God willing.

www.ingramcontent.com/pod-product-compliance
Lightning Source LLC
Chambersburg PA
CBHW071610080526
44588CB00010B/1080